Help! I'm a WOMAN IN YOUTH MINISTRY!

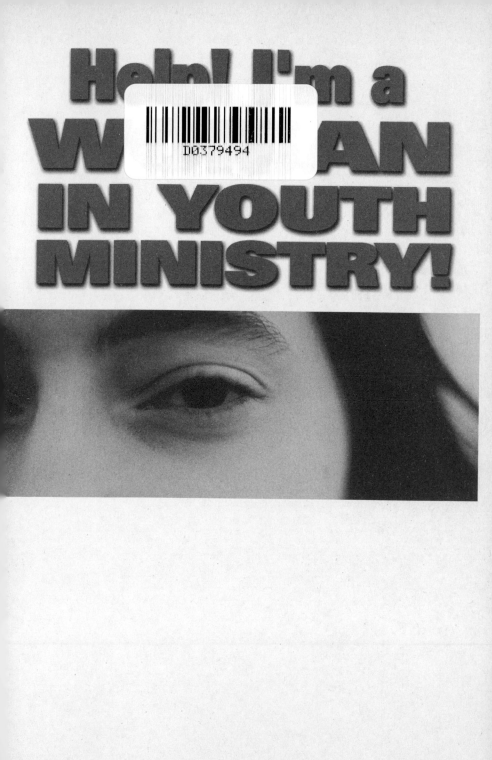

Help! I'm a WOMAN IN YOUTH MINISTRY!

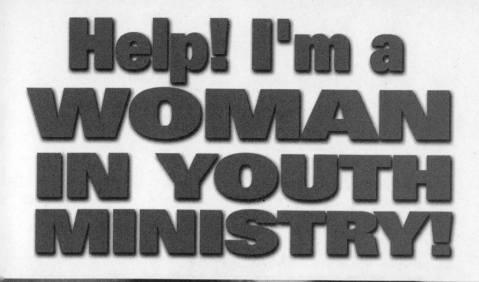

Practical Empowerment
for Your Calling and Your Life

KARA POWELL

WITH MEGAN HUTCHINSON AND HEATHER FLIES

Youth Specialties

www.youthspecialties.com

ZONDERVAN™

WWW.ZONDERVAN.COM

Help! I'm a Woman in Youth Ministry! Practical Empowerment for Your Calling and Your Life
Copyright © 2004 by Youth Specialties

Youth Specialties Books, 300 South Pierce Street, El Cajon, CA 92020, are published by
Zondervan, 5300 Patterson Avenue SE, Grand Rapids, MI 49530

Library of Congress Cataloging-in-Publication Data

Powell, Kara Eckmann, 1970-
  Help! I'm a woman in youth ministry! : practical empowerment for your
calling and your life / by Kara Powell, Heather Flies, and Megan
Hutchinson.
      p. cm.
Includes bibliographical references.
  ISBN 0-310-25552-X (pbk.)
  1. Church work with youth. 2. Women in church work. I. Flies,
Heather, 1973- II. Hutchinson, Megan, 1970- III. Title.
  BV4447.P655 2004
  259'.2--dc22
                                                                2003015151

Unless otherwise indicated, all Scripture quotations are taken from the Holy Bible: New
International Version (North American Edition), copyright © 1973, 1978, 1984 by
International Bible Society. Used by permission of Zondervan.

Web site addresses listed in this book were current at the time of publication. Please contact
Youth Specialties via e-mail (YS@YouthSpecialties.com) to report URLs that are no longer
operational and replacement URLs if available.

Edited by Laura Gross
Cover and interior design by Brian Smith
Printed in the United States

04 05 06 07 08 09 / DC / 10 9 8 7 6 5 4 3 2

To the women in youth ministry
who will someday mentor Nathan and Krista.

—Kara Powell

CONTENTS

INTRODUCTION

You probably want to keep reading this book if—
- Your body has more estrogen than testosterone,
- You care about teenagers,
- And you want to fall more in love with Jesus.

We've written this book with all sorts of women in mind:
- Professionals and volunteers,
- Rookies and veterans,
- Church and parachurch,
- Urban, suburban, and rural,
- From every denomination we could think of (as well as those who would rather not be part of any one denomination).

Our humble prayer is that God will use one—or maybe 21—of these ideas to give you roots deep in him and wings to take you to new ministry dreams.

Our Stories as Women in Youth Ministry

Dr. Kara Powell
(Executive Director of the Center for Ministry to Youth & Their Families at Fuller Theological Seminary; Coordinator of the Women's Youth Network; small group leader for student ministries at Lake Avenue Church in Pasadena, California)

My life as a woman in youth ministry has been a veritable "scratch and sniff" book. So many memories, so many thrills, each forever embedded in a vivid scent.

The smell of pizza reminds me of my time with students. All those Wednesday night dinners before church, summer pool parties, and overnighters are forever linked with the aromas of melted cheese, tomato sauce, olives, and pepperoni. In the midst of getting distracted by all the busyness and the business of youth ministry, pizza is my connection to the ultimate goal of all that hanging out: seeing students changed by Christ to change the world.

I love peanut butter; always have and always will (especially the crunchy kind). Part of what I love about it is that it's so portable, so easy to eat on the go. So when I think about my schedule as a woman in youth ministry, I smell peanut butter. Peanut butter and jelly (or my favorite variation: grilled peanut butter and jelly), peanut butter and apples, peanut butter and celery, and peanut butter on crackers have all been fuel as I've juggled the demands of students, volunteers, and families.

Since what I do flows out of who I am, my personal relationships have their own distinct scents in my "scratch and sniff" book. Every time I use my raspberry-scented lotion, my husband says, "Ahhh...Hawaii." During our honeymoon to Hawaii, I wore the lotion every day, and Dave says that when I wear it now, his mind is flooded with memories of our 10 days in Kauai. I like wearing it because it feels feminine. It helps me feel more like a woman and less like a Woman in Youth Ministry.

As a mom with a two year old and a four month old, all sorts of scents remind me of my kids (some of which are not too pleasant, even to me). But right now my two year old is enthralled by two things: Play-Doh and trains. I try to combine the two and make trains out of Play-Doh, complete with train tracks, bridges, and tunnels. In the midst of my love for youth ministry, the salty smell of Play-Doh reminds me of my primary disciples: my own kids.

May all the smells melt into an aroma that pleases my Father above.

Heather Flies

(Junior High Pastor at Wooddale Church in Eden Prairie, Minnesota; member of the Youth Specialties CORE training team; a popular youth rally emcee at school and church events)

My view of "women in ministry" is very different today than when I was growing up in a small-town, Baptist church. As I sat in the pew as a child and looked around, I saw women in the choir and at the piano or organ, but that was it. Sure, in the summer they would be busy making Rice Krispies Treats for the VBS kids down in the kitchen, but women were never seen speaking from the pulpit, handing out bulletins, or passing the offering plate. And it all seemed extremely normal to me.

When I entered Bethel College as a freshman, I met a woman named Sherry. She was articulate, wise, fun, AND the associate college pastor! Sherry was the first woman in ministry I had met. As we got to know each other, and she observed me, she said, "Heather, you're going to be in ministry." I kindly thanked her for her input and then reminded her of my plans to be the public relations director for the Minnesota Vikings and marry a defensive lineman. But both Sherry and the Lord continued to guide and affirm me in my ministry gifts and by my junior year, my communication major that was once chosen for the NFL was now redirected to communicating to kids and encouraging their hearts.

Today, I tell people I was knit together in my mother's womb to be a junior high pastor! My love for speaking, the Word, families, high-energy kids with braces, and leadership are a perfect fit for what God has called me to do. I am confident to stand before him one day and be held accountable for using my God-given gifts and the passion he instilled within me. By the way, I, too, love to make Rice Krispies Treats, but just try to keep me down in the kitchen (and away from kids)!

Megan Hutchinson

(Youth minister at Saddleback Church in Lake Forest, California; Director of Let's Talk About It; member of the Youth Specialties CORE training team)

My "calling" as a woman in youth ministry was both obvious and challenging. Obvious, because God couldn't have been more clear;

challenging because I was clueless about being a woman in what is predominantly a man's profession.

The obvious part was easy. I loved being around students. It energized me—still does. It is simply how God wired me. So I took the next logical step and began looking at women who did what I wanted to do: work full-time in youth ministry, speak, and write. I found these women had a few things in common. They felt called by God, loved students, and went to seminary. Convinced of the first two, off to seminary I went. And I absolutely loved it!

It was there I first encountered theological arguments for and against women in ministry. At first I was confused because I had not done any research. In fact, one night I was driving home while listening to Christian talk radio, and the host was asked, "If I am going to a church where a women, who is one of the best preachers I've ever heard, teaches periodically—should I leave?" Without hesitation the host said, "Absolutely! Leave right away. It is not biblical for a woman to teach."

I immediately pulled over on the side of the road and bawled my eyes out. "God," I cried, "You have given me the gift of teaching and evangelism. Why would you do this if it's unbiblical?" I felt frustrated and at times discouraged, but over time my answer would come.

Through much prayer and study, I have learned that women play a vital and important role in the ministry of the church. Although there are many opinions about the roles of women in ministry, you must stay true to how God specifically shaped you.

I've learned that for me, I am to be a wife first, then a mom, then a minister who teaches without reservation about the life-changing truths of the gospel of Christ. It's been quite a journey, but I've landed (do I hear an amen?). Today it is my prayer that I might "fearlessly make known" the gospel of Christ to all who may listen, be it male or female. My prayer is the same for you—that you would seek how God has specifically called you and go after that without reservation. I trust you will. Be encouraged!

SECTION ONE

YOU

YOU

What's Paul Got to Do With It?
Your Theology about Men and Women

As soon as I read these two words in the Ph.D. catalog, I knew it was the degree for me: practical theology. I had never seen the phrase before, but it immediately resonated with me. Some people joke that "practical theology" is an oxymoron, just like "military intelligence" or "jumbo shrimp." Instead, I counter that it's a redundancy. Our theology is inherently practical. Every aspect of our lives, from how

A couple of years ago, my husband Adam and I had the unique privilege of going to Israel. Naturally, we visited numerous sites we had read about in Scripture. One site in particular was an eye opener—a first-century synagogue in Capernaum where both Peter and Jesus taught. One of the things that struck me was the architecture. There was an upper galley where the women would sit and talk or gossip with their friends, and a lower level where the men would listen, intent on the message. Why is this? Because the men were educated, the women were not. Women living in the first century did not understand what was being taught, so they chatted with their friends throughout the service. Heck, I would too if I didn't have a clue what they were saying! I think that's why Paul wrote to Timothy that a woman should remain silent in the church. Today we are free to teach the wonderful truths of Scripture for we are now free to speak with the amazing gift of a theological education. Praise God!

—*Megan*

we treat the planet to how we treat other drivers, is shaped by what we think about God.

When it comes to women in ministry, our theology and our practices are intricately connected to one another. So if we're going to have better practices, we need better theology. Whether you're a theological novice or a veteran fluent in the original Greek, it's time to wrestle with the tough questions about women in leadership until you pin down some answers.

Start Local

Have you ever looked your senior pastor right in the eyes and asked him or her what they think about women in ministry? Are there any positions of leadership they think women shouldn't hold? If so, why? If not, why not? Make it your goal to listen, ask some questions, and then listen some more.

The Wesleyan Quad

John Wesley, the wise nineteenth-century pastor and theologian, taught that there are four ways to experience divine revelation: through Scripture, tradition, reason, and experience (see, I told you he was wise). We now call these four resources the Wesleyan Quadrilateral. When you're talking to folks about theology, try to see what side of the quadrilateral they use the most. Is it the Bible? Church tradition? Their own common sense? Or their own experience? Decide for yourself if any one side of the Quadrilateral is more important than the others, and weigh the evidence accordingly.

It's Greek to Me

How much time have you spent studying the key passages about women in leadership? Less time than you've spent shopping for shoes in the last month? If so, then it's time to bust out some books and do your homework.

There are two basic positions. On one extreme, the Complementarian view argues that while men and women are equal,

No matter what size church you come from, no one person can serve as THE youth pastor to all the students who attend. At our church we tell each small group leader — male or female — "You are a student's youth pastor, you are their shepherd." I've learned that regardless of job title, status, or gender, every student needs a pastor in their life to love on them, care for them, and ultimately show them Jesus.

— Megan

women have different leadership and teaching responsibilities in the church. On the other extreme, the Egalitarian view believes that gender does not influence divine call; God can (and does) call men and women to serve in any and every church leadership position.

Both sides are committed to the authority of Scripture. Both sides have tried to figure out the meaning of the original Hebrew Old Testament and Greek New Testament. The Complementarian view usually focuses on four texts, starting with 1 Corinthians 11:2-6, which teaches that the "head" of the woman is the man. Other primary texts are 1 Corinthians 14:33-35, which says women are to keep silent in the church; 1 Timothy 2:11-15, where keeping silent in the church is defined as refraining from teaching; and Ephesians 5:22-23, where Paul argues for different roles in a marriage.

The Egalitarian view also takes these texts seriously, but it begins from a different starting point. In Genesis 1–2, God makes both male and female in his image. In Genesis 3:16, the subordination of women is not prescribed as ideal, but rather predicted as a consequence of sin. Moving to the New Testament, in Galatians 3:28, Paul teaches that the hierarchies between Jew and Greek, slave and free, and male and female evaporate in light of Jesus Christ. In 1 Corinthians 11 and Acts 21:8-9, women are allowed to pray and prophesy in the early church. Given these texts, the Egalitarian view argues that the passages often used by the Complementarian view are heavily influenced by the particular culture involved in those epistles. Regulations on women in leadership are the exception, not the norm.

Which of these views is closest to your own? Why? Or do you have a completely different way of looking at it? Whatever you decide, your brain will be grateful for its aerobic workout.

Don't Know Much About History

An important principle in understanding scriptural passages about women in leadership is the principle of history. Divine revelation always occurs in the context of a specific culture. The ultimate divine revelation, Jesus himself, modeled this by entering into Palestinian culture and adopting its dress, language, and metaphors. For each city Paul wrote to in his epistles, take some time to understand the culture and their explicit and implicit guidelines for Jewish women. That knowledge just might unlock some of the mysteries that surround women in leadership.

Inside the Boundaries

What boundaries do you have for women in leadership? Are you comfortable with—

- Women serving in the background?
- Women meeting one on one with other girls or women?
- Women being small group leaders?
- Women "sharing" in front of a group?
- Women being teachers?
- Women being youth pastors?
- Women being senior pastors?
- Women being czars of the world?

Regardless of your answers, do your best to help women develop WITHIN those boundaries. Develop the best female small group leaders you can. Coach women how to speak to youth or to the entire church. Encourage girls to consider becoming senior pastors. Given the width of your boundaries, what can YOU do to encourage and empower women?

Start a Book Club

If you're like me, you learn best when you study alongside others. Invite some others to join you in a theological book club. Photocopy articles or swap relevant books about women in ministry and then meet monthly to discuss them. You might like it so much that you move to other topics and meet indefinitely.

Be Passionate, Not Mad

Once you've decided what you believe about women in youth ministry, let others know about it. But speak the truth in LOVE. In God's eyes, how you treat others who disagree with you is probably more important than whether or not you "win them over to your side."

Before I got married one of my heroes of the faith, Lori Salierno, said to me, "Megan, make sure you marry someone who wholeheartedly supports your role as a female in ministry...make sure he is your greatest cheerleader." A few years later, I met my Adam. Adam is my greatest cheerleader in ministry! In our six years of marriage, Adam has never held me back from my calling to kids. He empowers me to do exactly what God has led me to do without reservation. It is so freeing. I can't imagine doing what I do without his support and enthusiastic spirit. I dig that.

—Megan

Think Ahead

When preparing for a potentially difficult conversation, Abraham Lincoln spent a third of his time thinking about what he was going to say and two-thirds of his time thinking about what the other person was going to say. I can't think of better advice when it comes to talking about the theology of women in leadership. Know your own position, but also think ahead about what the other person might say. How would you respond to their position? What are its strong points? What are its potential weaknesses? Thinking this through in advance will bring greater depth to your conversation.

In the world of ministry, so much can happen in one day that I find I can talk and talk and TALK my husband's ear off without ever asking him, "Hey honey, how was your day...what's going on in your world?" Without pausing to ask this important question, it can often feel like it's all about me. (Which, let's face it, feels good sometimes, right?) But the truth is, checking in is a two-part deal, my deal and his. Be aware of the asking as well as the telling.

—*Megan*

Be Prepared for Mixed Messages

It's amazing how many men have "no theological problem" with women in leadership yet they "don't feel comfortable with it" themselves. Or vice versa—they want women to serve in leadership positions in their own ministries and churches, but they don't think Scripture supports it. While none of us is 100 percent consistent in our beliefs and actions, gently point out the mixed messages and see what they say. You might just start a great conversation.

Your First Family: Husbands and Children

What Do a PDA and a Pacifier Have in Common?

Do you know? Can you guess? Give up? Okay, I'll tell you—ME! For the last three years, the two items most vital to my very survival have been my Palm Pilot and a Nuk. I don't leave home without them. One keeps my schedule in order; one keeps my babies in order. Okay, Okay, pseudo-order.

If you have kids, this section will help you make sense of the topsy-turvy world of mom and ministry. And if you don't have kids yet, flip through the pages anyway. You know others who do. The moms of the girls you work with are hip deep in the delight and

My husband Adam is a hydro-geologist. Yep, you read it correctly, a hydro-geologist. In short, he works with water and rocks. While it took me two years to figure out what exactly he does, it also took me a while to figure out that his way of doing ministry and my way are different. At first I tried to have him do ministry the way I did. You know, just jump right in...connect with every student ...work the room! But I quickly recognized that while I was "connecting" with every student, he would connect with just one, and he could stay with that one for hours! It amazed me. Was he still doing ministry? You bet. It just looked different from they way I did it. But here's the amazing thing: youth ministry needs both types of people. I am an expert at making students feel welcomed; he's an expert at going deep with one. And together, it works!
—*Megan*

despair of family life. The more you understand them, the more you can speak their language. Plus, someday you might have your own kids, and it's never too soon to pick up a few pointers.

True/False: Marriage Hurts Your Ministry

I love asking college students this question. They almost always say true. Being married means less time out with students and fewer late-night donut runs. So yes, I spend about 30 percent less time with students now that I'm married.

But here's the catch: the time I spend is so much richer. Why? Because my relationship with my husband makes me a deeper person. So while I spend 30 percent less time with others, the time I do spend is doubly effective. So in reality, marriage CAN help your ministry. Do the math.

Check In Often

My husband and I talk three or four times each day while one or both of us are at work. I gather that's rare, but it shouldn't be. If we didn't touch base with each other during the day, then by the time I came home from my girls' small group at 9 p.m., I'd have to recap the whole day—starting with the fact that our two year old watched his first *Sesame Street* episode that morning and ending with the tough questions my girls asked about oral sex. I'd never remember everything, and I'd miss important details—about both our family and our ministry. Plus I'd get agitated or resentful that he wasn't with me to share it all. A few 10-minute phone calls each day make all the difference.

Your Husband's Calling

Since you're active in ministry, it's easy to forget that your husband has his own ministry calling. His call to work with two year olds, or international missions in Zimbabwe, or two year olds in Zimbabwe, can easily get pushed aside by the in-your-face demands of youth ministry. Make sure your husband is using his spiritual gifts in tangible ways every week. And if that means you go to one less Bible study or spend an hour less working on your Wednesday night talk, it's worth it—both for the kingdom and for your marriage.

My Husband Dislikes Youth Ministry

True confession time: My husband Dave, who is just about flawless, doesn't like junior high ministry. It's not that he doesn't believe in it; it's not that he doesn't think it's vital. It's just that he doesn't particularly like junior highers—at least not in large numbers. While he likes the girls in my small group when they come over to our house, junior highers in larger numbers scare him. When he walks into our junior high room, his spine stiffens and his voice changes. My husband, who can skillfully navigate his way through any executive

> **"When I hope** that the precious people in my life can exist without me, that's a sign of real trouble."
>
> —*Bill Hybels*

board meeting or complicated engineering procedure, gets freaked out by eighth graders.

If the same is true for your husband, that's okay. If your husband is like mine, he likes and loves YOU. He likes and loves that you are called to work with students. So while he may hardly ever peer into the youth room, he can still support you every minute before you step into that room and every minute after you step out of it. Pray together, strategize together, brainstorm together. Your husband can and should be your number one fan even if he's rarely in the room with you when you're doing ministry.

When I first started out in ministry,

I thought, "What a life! I can make my own hours, meet students when I want, and never bring 'work' home." I seriously separated church life and personal life. While this sounds lovely, it's totally ineffective. Why? Because working with students is life-on-life stuff. It's your world intersecting with the life of a teenager. It's allowing them to see you—really see you. This happens in the everyday stuff. Making dinner, running errands, changing dirty diapers, even allowing them to see you in the frustrating moments. That's the essence of the "Bring With" principle. Ever since I opened myself, my life, our home, and our family to students, ministry has never been so rich and effective!

—Megan

The "Bring With" Principle

One of my favorite verses about ministry comes from the Apostle Paul. He writes to the people in 1 Thessalonians 2:8 that he loved the Thessalonians so much that he shared more than just the gospel, he shared his very life.

I love that phrase: "our very lives." As much as you can, combine your time spent with teenagers with family time. Do you have to go grocery shopping? Invite someone you're mentoring to go with you. Are you going to spend an hour at your nine-year-old's soccer game? Take a teenager with you. Not only are they spending time with you, but they're also seeing your family in action. And depending on their family background, that might be even more valuable to them than time spent alone with you.

"I Don't Know How You Do It"

Have those words ever been directed at you? "I don't know how you do it." A husband, kids (your own, not the students), more kids (the students, not your own), a house to manage, a career to build, a family calendar to keep, friends to maintain…just making the list is exhausting, let alone living it.

More than most, Kate Redman knows just how exhausting it can be. She's the fictional character in Allison Pearson's hit novel, *I Don't Know How She Does It*. The opening scene captures the tension between the job you do in your house and the job you do outside of it.

> Monday, 1:37 a.m. How did I get here? Can someone please tell me that? Not this kitchen. I mean in this life. It is the morning of the school carol concert, and I am hitting mince pies. No, let us be quite clear about this, I am *distressing* mince pies, an altogether more demanding and subtle process.
>
> Discarding the luxury packaging, I winkle the (store bought) pies out of their pleated foil cups, place them on a chopping board and bring down a rolling pin on their blameless floury faces. This is not as easy as it sounds, believe me. Hit the pies too hard and they drop a kind of fat-lady curtsy, skirts of pastry bulging out at the sides, and the fruit starts to ooze. But with a firm downward motion— imagine enough pressure to crush a small beetle—you can start a crumbly little landslide, giving the pastry a pleasing homemade appearance. And homemade is what I'm after

here. Home is where the heart is. Home is where the good mother is, baking for her children.[1]

I wish I could sit down with Kate over Mocha Frosted Lattes and tell her that the pace she's trying (emphasis on *trying*) to keep is insanity. That she can only be great, truly great, in a few things. Pick those few things wisely, and let everything else slide. If you bring store-bought desserts to your child's school (or—gasp, shudder—no dessert at all), who cares? In the light of eternity, does it really matter if you have Lego Duplo blocks strewn around your living room and your kid's bacteria colony science project sprawled across your dining room table when the in-laws come over? I want to be a great lover of Jesus, Dave, and my kids (in that order). Everything else is just gravy.

Creative Ways to Get a Few Hours with Your Kids

With 24 hours a day, seven nights a week, and two days off a week, why is it still so hard to find time with your own kids? Here are a few ideas to get you some quality and quantity time with your family.

Couch Time

Ever since I can remember, my husband and I have had Couch Time. What exactly is it? It's the first 15 minutes after he walks through the door after work. Mellow music is often playing in the background and we sit on our comfy couch for 15 minutes unwinding and hugging. It's wonderful! Sound unrealistic? I dare you to try it! Your kids may think you've lost your marbles at first, but slowly they will learn that this is "mommy and daddy time" and adjust accordingly. There is nothing more comforting to a child than to know mom and dad are secure, in love, and solid. NOTHING. Couch time is just 15 minutes! Try it for a couple weeks. I dare you.

—*Megan*

Ditch Day

Skip church sometime. Just ditch. Take your kids to a park, a mall, or out for ice cream instead. Don't run errands. Don't nag. And don't lecture. Talk, laugh, ask questions, and listen. You'll probably feel guilty for skipping church. But that's your own hyperactive I-gotta-serve gland. Don't be so busy ministering to other people's kids that you end up forgetting your own. Please.

Date Night—with Your Kids

Set aside a night every week as date night. Sometimes your family can do one event together; other times you can split up the kids between you and your husband. Let the kids choose what you're going to do. And then do it—without checking your watch or making calls on your cell phone.

An Hour a Week

Set an appointment with each of your kids for an hour per week. They choose what you do together: basketball, Barbies, and banana splits—they're all fair game.

Birthday Dates

Every month, take your child out for a special treat on the date of her birthday. For example, if she was born on September 20, then on the twentieth of every month, take her out for a donut before school, an ice cream after school, or a burrito for dinner. This way you know that every month you'll have face time with each of your children.

Family Vacations

When my younger brother got married, I wrote him a letter (a long letter) explaining what I appreciated about him and listing some of my fondest memories of our time together. Over two-thirds of those memories came from family vacations. We lived together, ate together, and shared a bathroom 365 days per year, but what really stands out is playing "go fish" in Yosemite, destroying an inflatable raft in Hawaii, and his smelly shoes in France. Plan ahead and schedule a few family vacations every year. If money is tight, go camping or stay with friends. But get away.

Creativity at Home

Why is it that we can come up with all these great party ideas and games for our youth ministry, but then we eat the same pasta in the same boring dining room night after night at home? It's too bad we exhaust our creativity bank account with our youth group so we are bankrupt when we walk into our own house. Think about fun things you do with your youth group and try them with your own kids. Go with your kids to kidnap a friend for breakfast in their pajamas, surprise your kids by inviting their friends over for dinner, or bake cookies (or brownies if you're really short on time) and deliver them to your kids' friends. Show your kids that your zany ideas are for family, too.

The 15-Minute Housecleaning Rule

Have you been meaning to clean out your refrigerator but don't have the time? Are you still wearing shorts in December because you haven't had time to bring out your winter clothes and put away your summer outfits? Start breaking down your housecleaning jobs into 15-minute increments. Sure, you don't have the 45 minutes you need to properly clean out your refrigerator, but you might have 15 minutes while the taco meat is simmering to clean out the fruit and vegetable drawers. You don't have the hour you need to sort through your entire dresser, but you do have 10 minutes to organize your socks. Ten minutes here; 15 minutes there; it all adds up to a cleaner and calmer home.

1-800-GOODWILL

I used to hate cleaning out my house because I'd end up with bags full of donations for Goodwill. Having no place to store the bags, they'd end up stacked on top of my husband's tools in the garage. For months. Until finally my husband couldn't take it anymore and he'd drag the bags in front of the house for anyone to take.

But all that changed when I learned that Goodwill is willing to come to our house ANY time to pick up donations. You probably have an Amvets, a Disabled Veterans Organization, or a Goodwill center in your area that provides the same service. Now I have one area in the garage where we put our donations, then every few months I call Goodwill and they come a day or two later. Much better for our garage. Much better for our marriage.

The Mighty Crockpot

If you do NOTHING else in this book, trying this one tip will save you one to two hours per week. Buy a slow-cooker. Get some recipes, either from a cookbook or from Crockpot recipe Web sites. In 10 minutes you can slice up the food, shove it in the slow-cooker, and then leave it alone for four to eight hours until *Voila!* Dinner is ready. And it's almost always enough dinner for two evenings. Some people say the food is too mushy, or it all tastes like carrots, but hey, for two inexpensive, healthy dinners in 10 minutes, I can grow pretty fond of mush and carrots.

Light a Candle

The ONLY thing I like about the time change in the fall, when it gets dark around 5:30 p.m., is candlelight dinners. For the price of a $5 candle and the seven seconds it takes to light the candle, our family gains a more relaxing atmosphere. The kids are better behaved, we have deeper conversations, and we linger longer over dinner.

Sixty Minutes and Some Java

Even when you've had one of those no-good-rotten-terrible-very-bad days, almost everything gets better when you spend an hour in a coffee house. Go late at night when your husband gets home, or pay for day-care for that hour. But grab a book and get some time for yourself. (I should know. I'm sitting at my favorite coffee house as I write this.)

Your Own Bridget Jones Diary: Being a Single Woman in Youth Ministry

My single friend once summarized, "Life is like swimming laps. Married women have their husbands and families as floatation devices. They go slower, but they can stay afloat longer. Single women are sleek and can glide through the water faster. But without the floaties, their arms get pretty tired."

As a former single person (and a former swimmer), I could relate to her metaphor. And if you're single, you probably can, too. You've got a more flexible schedule and more time to pursue your own interests, but along with the freedom extra loneliness and insecurities creep in. May the following words be part of the divine water wings you need to stay afloat.

Understand Where to Put the Dash

Single women in youth ministry tend to fall into three categories. The first consists of women who are in "single doubt." They have doubts about themselves, wondering if there's something "wrong" with them because they aren't married yet.

The second category consists of women who are "singled-out." In a culture that often revolves around marriage, they wonder if being different means being less valuable.

The third consists of women who are "singled out." They understand that God has selected them to be single. And whether they remain single for another month or their entire lifetime, they know they have a divine calling to serve God and others in every chapter of their lives. They've found that when God calls, he always provides, and that includes meeting their needs for intimacy and growth.

When I was single, I waffled back and forth among all three categories. But the more I stayed in the first two, the more miserable I made myself. Ask God to help you savor your singleness and treasure the wisdom of Mennonite theologian John H. Yoder: "Marriage is not wrong, and existing marriages are to be nurtured. Yet there exists no Christian imperative to become married as soon as one can or to prefer marriage over singleness as a more whole or wholesome situation...It needs to be taught as normative Christian truth that singleness is the first normal state for every Christian."

Finding Contentment in Your Own Pasture

Ever look at the married women in your life and wish you were where they are? Ever long to experience life as they do? During my single years, I felt like I had ALL this love in my heart and no one to receive it.

At that same time, I discovered words that would change my life, "Trust in the Lord and do good; dwell in the land and enjoy safe pasture. Delight yourself in the Lord and He will give you the desires of your heart" (Psalm 37:3,4). Through these verses, the Lord showed me that the "single pasture" he had me in was exactly where he wanted me.

As I was plastered up against the fence of my pasture, looking longingly into the pastures of my friends, the Lord gently whispered, "Heather, turn around." And when I did, what I saw was a generation of kids who longed to experience the love that was overflowing in my heart. It was then that my "full-time" job changed—instead of longing to be in the pastures of others, I committed to exploring every blade of grass in mine until God chose to swing open the gate and lead me into a new pasture of life.

—Heather

Singleness Awareness Day

Okay, sure, Valentine's Day is a hard day. While it means flowers and romance for couples, it's a certified Singleness Awareness Day for singles. But the good thing about this particular holiday is that singles tend to bond together, holding impromptu movie nights and pizza parties.

It's the other Singleness Awareness Days that are really hard: weddings, work parties, Christmas parties—those "bring-a-date" occasions. Your two best options: invite someone or walk into that room wearing the confidence that comes from knowing Jesus. You are HIS beloved. And that makes a lot of difference.

> **When I first entered ministry** as a part-timer, the only answer I seemed to know was "Yes!" As a single woman, I would take on responsibilities with less than 24 hour's notice, be the last one to leave the church at night, be the first one there in the morning, adjust vacation plans to accommodate programs, and stay at the office until 2 a.m. just to "get a few more things done." And in a warped sense, I felt good about it all—like I was a better minister or a better Christian because of those sacrifices.
>
> Eventually, I hit a wall. Hard. I was exhausted, drained, discouraged, and had no idea how to ignite the passion for ministry that used to burn so brightly. It was during this time of desperation and fear that "Heather Time" was created. I opened my planner and began to block out three-hour blocks at least every other day. If there were no three-hour blocks available, I would boldly cancel what was in the way of those blocks.
>
> Now as a full-time, married minister, that time is even more essential, and I'm so thankful I started that healthy pattern early on in my ministry! I am certain it is my "Heather Time" that has allowed me to continue passionately in ministry for 12 years!
>
> —*Heather*

A Surrogate Spouse

When you're single, it's all too easy to make the ministry your surrogate spouse. When you feel lonely, you call up a kid. When you have a free Friday night, you buy some brownie mix and have a youth group slumber party. When the pastor needs someone to do some extra work, you volunteer because hey—you don't have a family to go home to.

While that's okay sometimes, if it becomes a pattern, you might need to set up some boundaries that give you a personal life beyond your ministry. After all, there's a big difference between being used by God and just being used up.

Have Adult Friends

In the last month how much time have you spent with teenagers? How much time have you spent with people your own age? (And no, staying to clean up after Wednesday night youth group with the rest of the staff doesn't count.) What do these two numbers tell you about yourself? Are you so busy with kids that you've lost track of your own peers? If so, give yourself a sabbatical from teenagers and hook up with some of your girlfriends.

Sex and the Single Woman

A speaker once joked that "Sex and the Single" was the shortest seminar he had ever done. If that's true, he doesn't know much about singleness…or sexuality. Being single doesn't mean you lack a "sex life." You have the same hormones and desires as married women. What's missing is an appropriate outlet.

I've seen single women in youth ministry develop close friendships with some of the older guys in high school. They claim they're like an "older sister" who is there to listen and support the guys, but I've often wondered (and sometimes asked!) if they're getting their needs for intimacy and cross-gender relationships fulfilled in unhealthy ways.

Don't fool yourself. Are you a bit too close to some of the guys in your group, especially the juniors and seniors? Are you relying on them for male attention, maybe even flirting with them a bit to provoke it? If so, then talk to a trusted female confidante. Distance yourself from the guys involved. God's got something way better for them and for you.

Beware the Blind Date

As she's picking up Juaneta from youth group, Juaneta's mom yells out the car window, "I know a great guy for you. Do you want me to set you up?"

You shrug and say, "Sure," and the next thing you know, you're sharing a glamorous night at Denny's with a guy who's 15 years older than you and reminds you more of your dad than a date.

Sound familiar? If so, then you're part of the growing club of Single Women in Youth Ministry Who Have Had Really Bad Blind Dates. The next time someone asks you if you want to go out with that great coworker/neighbor/cousin, ask a few follow-up questions: How old is he? What does he like to do? What's his relationship with God like? What kind of ministry is he involved in? And here's a biggie: Why do you think we'd be good for each other?

But Aren't Guys Going to Be Intimidated By Me?

Before I got married, I used to be worried that guys would be intimidated by me since I was a youth leader. My fears were somewhat justified. A few guys who approached me in coffee houses changed their tune when they asked me what I was reading, and I told them I was studying New Testament Greek.

But here's what I learned. If a guy is intimidated by you, then he's probably not the right guy for you. That doesn't mean you should go out of your way to act like a Big Bad Woman in Youth Ministry, but it does mean you should be yourself—calling and all. And if a guy is not attracted to that, he's not worth the time.

Since You're Not Supporting a Family...

Many women who get paid by their church to do youth ministry have heard something like this: "We so appreciate your ministry here, and we'd like to pay you more. But things are tight. And after all, it's not like you're supporting a family."

Ugh. Double ugh. First off, it's not legal. Second, someday you might get married and need to support a family and could really use a nest egg. Third, if you don't ever get married, you will probably need an even bigger nest egg because the only one tossing money toward the nest is you. Ask to be paid according to the salary scale set up by the church for the rest of its employees. Whether or not you've got a ring on your finger shouldn't make a difference in your paycheck.

Don't Push the Pause Button

Do you have a list of things you'll do "once you get married"? Backpack through Europe, buy tickets to the Super Bowl, climb Mount Whitney? Are any of those things really going to be more likely to happen once you get married and have more responsibilities? Probably not.

So why wait? Get a few friends, save up some money, and step out into adventure. Not only is it good for you, but it's good for your students. They'll learn that being single doesn't mean you have to push the pause button on your life.

Adopt a Family

Which TV family offers the most realistic view of family life for your students' families?

A. The Osbournes

B. The Bradys

C. The Simpsons

D. The Huxtables

E. The Gilmores (from The WB's *Gilmore Girls*)

F. The Lopezes (from ABC's *The George Lopez Show*)

G. The Hennessys (from ABC's *8 Simple Rules*)

How about none of the above?

It's easy to glamorize married life. From the island of the single woman, the island of the married woman seems like a cross between Hawaii and Tahiti. But it's not. And you need to know that.

Get close to the families of your students, especially the female students. Invite yourself over to dinner. Volunteer to come over some Saturday morning to help pull weeds. In the midst of the meals and the crabgrass, you'll see that family life is no bed of roses.

During my college years, I so desired to have a companion. I had plenty of great friends, but this longing was different. From the first moment I began noticing boys, I developed a list of standards for the one I would choose someday. But after years of not dating, the people around me hinted that maybe my standards were just a little too high. I started to listen to the hints.

It was those voices that moved me to consider a guy named Kyle. Kyle had been pursuing me for over a year but I had no interest in him. He struggled with his temper and lacked fashion sense; he wasn't excited about my ministry; and when I thought about kissing him, I would begin to dry-heave. But as I looked around, no one else was looking my way, so I gave in to the hints of others and to Kyle. What followed were two dates and a year of misery as I tried to convince him that I was not the one for him.

Friends, no matter how deeply you long for someone to share life and laughter with, don't lower the standards God has laid on your heart! Genesis 2:18 tells us that God created a "suitable helper" for Adam—someone fashioned just for him. Knowing that, why do so many of us wander over to the "clearance racks" of men to search for "the one"? As women who were knit together in our mother's womb by our Creator, we deserve so much more than a blue-light special!

—Heather

Know Where You Fall on the Vulnerability Spectrum

Some single women in youth ministry are very tightlipped about their dating lives. They figure it's none of their students' business, and they don't want to drag their kids through the ups and downs of their romances. Other single women are regular *National Enquirers,* sharing with students what they like and don't like about their dates all in the name of being "real."

Which extreme do you fall into? And what can you do about it? If you keep your dating cards a little too close to your vest, then let students know a little more about the guys you're dating. Ask them to pray for wisdom as you're getting to know different guys. And if you're more of a "tell all," make it your motto to just tell some. Ask yourself if you'd be sharing the same information if your students' parents were sitting there with you. If not, then you should probably keep your mouth shut.

Controlling Your PDA So It Doesn't Control You

Take your best guess at filling in the blank below:

> Your view of _____ and use of it will tell more about you...than almost anything else. It is not an extra in life, but it is the medium in which all that we see, hear, feel, imagine, think, judge and do takes place.

Got any guesses? Would it be easier if I told you this quote came from a book by Robert Banks called *The Tyranny of Time?*

Our time is our most valuable commodity. It's one of the few things where once we use it, we can never get it back. It's one of God's greatest gifts to us, and one of our daily questions should be: How can I best use the divine gift of the next 24 hours? As women in youth ministry, there are all sorts of answers to that question. Your answer is certain to be different from mine. Your answer about Tuesday is probably different than your answer for Friday. Whether you face a day of diaper duty or back-to-back meetings, this section will help you unwrap some common themes about schedules and organize your calendar around them.

True or False Test

In *When I Relax I Feel Guilty* (don't you dig the title?), Tim Hansel identifies several myths we have about the importance of work in our schedule. Read the list below and circle the myths that are near and dear to *your* heart.

1. Work is the primary source of my identity.

2. Work is inherently good, and therefore, the more work I do, the better person I am.

3. I am not really serving the Lord unless I consistently push to the point of fatigue.

4. The more I work, the more God loves me.

5. If I work hard enough 50 weeks a year, then I "deserve" a vacation.

6. Most of my problems would be solved if I would only work harder.[2]

As I was reading this list a few years ago, I glanced over at my newborn son. Nathan's grand daily accomplishment as a three month old: filling his diapers. And yet I loved him more than I ever thought I would or could. That's how God feels about you. You are his beloved. Your work is irrelevant to his love.

I'll Get Some Rest When the Work Is Done

Maybe you live in a more utopian world than I do, but there is always one more student in crisis, one more talk to fine-tune, or one—or 21—more e-mails to return. Being a youth worker, and being a follower of Christ for that matter, means our work is never done. And yet we live as if things will improve if we just work harder.

Think of Jesus. When he moved into the Jewish neighborhood, he was inundated by all sorts of people with all sorts of needs. And what did he do? *WWJD*? Not heal everyone, that's what.

If I Rest, People Will Think I'm Lazy

If you care about impressing other people, you probably shouldn't be in youth ministry in the first place. Your primary audience is not other people or yourself, but your Father in heaven.

Plus, you have it backward: Busyness is actually a sign of laziness. It shows that you don't have the strength and the will to go against our culture. Letting others decide your agenda, thereby avoiding the excruciating choices of setting priorities for what you're going to do and—more importantly—for what you're NOT going to do, makes you *more* lazy, not less.

Growing up as an outspoken, extroverted, energetic, and articulate leader, I was always asked to fill roles of responsibility. It started in kindergarten when I was given the honor of being a line leader. It continued through elementary school where I was a peer counselor and a member of the school patrol. High school brought on the roles of alto section leader, student council class president, president of SADD, and speaker for SHOC (an anti-drug and alcohol committee). I won't even get into my college years!

As I matured, I began to understand that because of how God created me, I would never be at a loss for things to do and ministries to be a part of, but I was not the only one God could use to further that ministry, encourage that kid, or solve that world problem. And that, my friends, was the first step in recovering from my "savior syndrome." I realized that not only was I overdoing it, but there was also the possibility that I was taking someone else's space in the body of Christ—someone who could have filled that spot more effectively.

—Heather

If I Stop Working, How Will the Work Get Done?

This is undoubtedly my most insidious obstacle to put to rest. Who is the ultimate worker? Who is the ultimate pastor? Like you, I am a shepherd (with a lower case s) over students but our Father is their ultimate Shepherd (with a capital S). We aren't part of a tag team with God. It's not like it's my turn for a while, and then when I get tired, I reach out my hand, touch his, and it's his turn to dive into the ring. It's ALWAYS his turn.

> **"Fatigue** makes cowards of us all."
> — *Vince Lombardi, football coach*

Number Four on God's Top Ten

Don't you just love holidays? And I'm not just talking about the big three: Easter, Thanksgiving, and Christmas. I mean those other Monday ones: Memorial Day, Labor Day, and Veterans Day. Twenty-four hours without a job. Twenty-four hours to rest and relax. Twenty-four hours to spend with the friends and family you care about.

What if I told you that the God of the universe wants you to have 24 hours like that every week?

As a woman in youth ministry, you may have successfully side-stepped the more obvious landmines of sexual immorality, lying, and cheating on your taxes, but check out commandment number four in God's original Top Ten list in Exodus 20:8-10: "Remember the Sabbath day by keeping it holy. Six days you shall labor and do all your work, but the seventh day is a Sabbath to the Lord your God." Female youth workers violate this commandment more than any other.

I suppose I've been marinating in the Protestant Work Ethic much of my life. I've learned that work is good. Work is holy. Work is what God wants me to do. As long as I can keep myself from getting sick, what difference does it make if I work and study 70 to 80 hours a week? Until I ventured into a commitment to a weekly

---

We have special toll roads in California. The idea is if you take them, you get there faster. One day I'm driving, and I see in big huge font: "WE DON'T SLOW DOWN, WHY SHOULD YOU?" At that, my jaw dropped. I'll tell you why I *should* slow down: Because when I don't, I'm impatient rather than calm, controlling and not gentle, irritable versus steady and predictable, a reactionary rather than a compassionate responder. *That's why*! Rest changes me. And you, too.

— *Megan*

Sabbath a few years ago, I had no idea what I had been missing. How can I enter the quiet place beside the still waters unless I stop? How can I lead others into the quiet place beside the still waters if I am in perpetual motion?

If You Want to Have Your Own Sabbath, Here Are Some Tips to Keep in Mind:

- The Sabbath is more about New Testament freedom than Old Testament law. Jesus abolished Sabbath legalism, NOT the practice of the Sabbath. Instead, he actually elevated its importance by calling himself the "Lord of the Sabbath" (Matthew 12:1-8). If you're avoiding the Sabbath, you may actually be stepping into the same kind of legalism as the first century Pharisees. After all, what is the root of legalism? It's thinking that you have to EARN salvation. Many women in youth ministry are avoiding the Sabbath with the same underlying motive: thinking that we have to EARN God's approval.

- Each week look ahead on your calendar and block out some time by writing the word *Sabbath* on it. After all, the Sabbath won't automatically appear in your calendar. You have to intentionally schedule it. No one will do it for you.

- When in Sabbath, PRAY and PLAY.[3] A good Sabbath has meaningful times of worship, prayer, journaling, and meditation

I met a female youth worker who said her boss wouldn't allow a full day off for anyone. "Ministry needs us," he'd say. I looked her straight in the eye and said, "Quit your job." She thought I was crazy at first but then realized she worked for a workaholic dressed in sheep's clothing. She went back and showed him the passages of Scripture where Jesus clearly rested, and he fired her.

—Megan

balanced with time spent hanging out with friends, taking a hike, or reading a gripping novel.

- Set aside as much time as you can, even if it's just a half-day. Or a few hours. There are times in my life where ministry demands or family commitments make an entire day of rest impossible. On those weeks, I try to set aside a half-day. Or three hours. Whatever I can get. And if you have kids, you may have to swap children with another family to get some quality time, meaning you take a Sabbath every other week.

- Avoid items on your to-do list like the plague. It's tempting to "accidentally" do something that is actually work (i.e., cleaning your garage, buying a birthday gift for your brother, sorting your clothes) on your Sabbath day. As much as possible, try to

All the pastors at my church are allowed one-and-a-half days off each week. Because Sunday, which is a normal day off for most of the nation, is one of our busiest days of ministry, we end up taking our Sabbath on another day. When I first started as the junior high pastor, I tried to take my day and a half. I would look at my planner on Monday and think, Which day can I take off this week? What I saw before me were appointments, programs, and events that spanned all of my days. Well, I would say to myself, I'll just be sure I get one next week. It never happened.

Last year, I got smart. I went to the month of September in my Palm Pilot and marked every single Thursday as "Day Off." In addition, I communicated to my coworkers, volunteer staff, and junior high families that from now on Thursdays were going to be my Sabbath. I was encouraged (and even a little shocked!) when everyone responded with things like "Good for you!" or "I'm proud of you!"

On those crazy weeks when life seems out of control, I look toward my Sabbath day and say, "I can make it to Thursday!"

—Heather

stick to activities that truly refresh and restore you. You've got the other six days to do everything else. You might want to try one of my traditions—taking a nap. Sleeping is actually an incredible act of faith. When I sleep during the day, I'm saying, "God, I trust you to take care of things until I wake up."

• Talk openly about what you're doing with students, friends, and the people at your church. We in ministry have done a fantastic job of infecting each other with pseudo-workaholism camouflaged as dedication. Wouldn't it be great if we could turn the tables and infect each other with a commitment to biblical rest and refreshment? Wouldn't it be great if when someone approached you in your church lobby and asked, "So, are you keeping busy?" and you could honestly say, "No, not really"? And when you said "no," you didn't have to worry about being judged or ridiculed? The early church fathers would have told you that being busy was a sin. How did a vice become a virtue?

Get a New Scale

As women in youth ministry, it's easy to evaluate our days by how much we got done. If we made good progress on our talk, finished up registration for the mission trip, had a few good conversations with students, and answered all our e-mails, we feel like we had a productive day. If not, we feel bad about our days and ourselves.

Where does the Bible say that we should judge our days based on how much we do? Jesus actually says the opposite. Our two priorities are to love God and to love others. So try using how much you love God and how much you love people as the scales to measure each day.

Priority Grid

It was one of those days. I felt so overwhelmed and so busy that I didn't even feel like I had time to go to the bathroom (you know what I mean, don't you?). I was sharing my anxiety with my husband, Dave, over dinner, and he—being the engineer that he is— suggested I try something called a Priority Grid. It's something he made up, but here's how it works.

Side B

Things I like to do...			
Totals			

Side A

Start by writing the list of items you want to prioritize (i.e., your roles or "to-do" tasks) in the column of shaded boxes on the left side of the chart (we'll call it "Side A"). Next, write the same list of things in the row of shaded boxes across the top (we'll call this "Side B").

Starting with the item listed in the first shaded box on Side A, compare it to each item listed in the Side B boxes, asking yourself which of the two things is more important. If the item or task from Side A is more important, write a zero in the box between the two items. If the Side B item is more important, then write a one. When the first row is complete, start again using the item written in the second shaded box in the Side A column.

When you have filled in every box, total the numbers for each column and write the totals in the row at the bottom of the chart. The Side B items with the highest totals should also have a higher priority in your life.

Here's an example:

Side B

Things I like to do...	Kiss my spouse	Fix plumbing	Make dinner
Kiss my spouse	1	0	0
Fix plumbing	1	1	1
Make dinner	1	0	1
Totals	3	1	2

Side A

I try to do this every month or two; and when I do, it quickly shows me where I should focus my energy and what I should consider dropping from my schedule. (Clearly, I need to kiss my spouse!)

This prioritization exercise takes 10 to 15 minutes to do, but it's saved me hundreds of hours.

Get a Hobby

What do you do for fun? And no, hanging out at high school track meets doesn't count. Let me rephrase the question—What do you do for fun that has nothing to do with making you a better youth worker? Are you stumped? Then you need a hobby. Take a dance class. Borrow a mountain bike. Become a pasta aficionado. Develop a piece of your life that is yours alone.

Work Out

This is probably not the first time you've heard this, but physical exercise is essential for your physical, emotional, mental, and even spiritual health. Yet on lots of days the last thing I want to do is throw on my Adidas, load my kids in the stroller, and walk around our neighborhood.

But I do. Why? Because I tell myself that when I'm done, I'll be glad I did it. My mind feels sharp, my body feels strong, and my emotions feel balanced.

Ask yourself: have you ever regretted exercising? Probably not. So find something that fits in your schedule and budget (yoga, lifting weights, swimming, joining a soccer league, finding a walking partner), lace up those tennis shoes, and work up a sweat.

Fifteen-Minute Relaxer

Have you discovered something you can do in 15 minutes that totally relaxes you? Does pulling weeds calm your nerves? Does picking up the phone and calling an old friend from college soothe your soul? For me, 15 quiet minutes in the bathtub make all the difference. So figure out something that will relax you in 10 to 15 minutes, and give yourself the freedom to indulge in that activity *whenever* you need a break. Being relaxed is one of the *best* gifts you can give to the friends, family, and students you care about. By taking care of yourself, you're taking care of them, too.

My Tuesdays are nutty. I wake up at 6 a.m., leave the house by 8 a.m., go to every meeting under the sun, and then meet with my student small group until 9:30 p.m. It's a whirlwind of a day. However, I've recently figured out a method to survive this chaotic day. In my Palm Pilot I put the word *relax* at 4:30 p.m. Once the alarm goes off, it takes me about a half hour to leave the office, but by 5 I am home RELAXING in the bathtub for 15 minutes—bubbles and all. I light a candle, turn off the phone, and soak, soak, soak. Then around 5:30 p.m., I'm dressed and ready to head out, only now I feel like my tank is full again because I pushed the pause button in the middle of it all.

—Megan

A One-to-One Comparison

For too long, I've squeezed too many things into my schedule because, after all, "It's only an hour meeting" or "That student really needs someone to talk to." While that may be true, I've now started to view my time in a one-to-one comparison. When I compare that one-hour meeting to an hour with my family, is it worth it? When I compare time with that student to time playing trains on the living room carpet with my kids, which is the better use of time? When you make such a direct comparison, your priorities rise to the top. Quickly.

Beneath the Façade: Temptations and Insecurities

I Am Woman! Hear Me Roar!

Well, okay…some days. Other days I feel more like a mouse than a lion. Why is it that some days I feel confident in my calling and relish the opportunity to minister to students while other days I am paranoid about what others are thinking of me and would rather just stay in bed? If we're honest with ourselves, each of us has our own long list of temptations and insecurities that paralyze us. And sometimes the items on our lists seem to contradict each other: pride one day, insecurity the next, grandiosity on Monday, self-loathing on Tuesday.

The bad news is that because of our sin, we will never be able to fully break free from our temptations and insecurities. But as we'll see in this section, the good news is that because of God's grace, we can at least make some baby steps. After all, three steps forward and two steps back is still one step forward.

At Best, We Feel Different; At Worst, We Feel Isolated

Being a woman in youth ministry is a lot like the Where's Waldo book series. You feel like you're different than the rest. Stating the obvious, you're different than the men you work with (see sections three and four for more on that topic).

And while you probably have some amazing female friends, if they haven't sat crying with a heartbroken seventeen year old or had smushed glazed donuts at 6 a.m. after an all-nighter, they don't get all of you.

When I first realized I was headed for youth ministry, I began looking for "female heroes" who had gone before me. One was all I needed. Her name was Lori Salierno, and she was actually doing it! She was out there, teaching men and woman, young and old, hands-on youth ministry. So I took a risk and phoned her. She was wonderfully responsive and soon thereafter, we actually met! She basically said, "In the male dominated culture of youth ministry, you'll need to do all you can to be worth your salt. Go to seminary. Take every opportunity you know. Don't be afraid to get your hands dirty. Go and do what other people won't. Be willing, get educated, and pray, pray, pray for God to lead you directly according to his path. And remember, 'He who called you IS faithful'...Let's stick together." This moment was the beginning of me finding another Waldo in my world. It felt great!

—*Megan*

At worst, those feelings of being different evolve into feeling isolated. It's tempting to let ourselves withdraw more and more into our "You Just Don't Get Me" corner. Don't stay there long. (Flip to section two of this book, which covers networking, for more help.)

A 1998 survey of 2,400 youth workers in multiple denominations revealed that female youth workers are more likely than males to feel unqualified.[4] Maybe we truly are less qualified, but I think it's more likely that we are just as qualified, but we just don't realize it.

Mixed Messages

As women leaders, we are sent all sorts of mixed messages:

Be on top of things, but not too nitpicky on details.

Be in touch with your feminine side, but not too prissy.

Be smart, but not too smart.

Use your gifts, but not too publicly.

Be strong, but not intimidating.

Be attractive, but not distracting to the men you partner with.

Be nice, but not wimpy.

Messages like these are enough to make a girl's head spin—especially if she doesn't have someone to talk to about it. Find another woman (ideally a youth worker) and talk about the mixed messages you struggle with. Invite her to tell you if you are being too nice or not nice enough, too strong or not strong enough—even if others just perceive you that way. Your character will be deepened and so will your impact.

Between a Wimp and a Witch

One of my biggest prayers for myself is that I would be a woman of "gentle strength." Why do I believe gentle strength is so important? First, Jesus modeled it for us. He wept with compassion, yet he overturned tables in the temple. He mourned over the death of his friend, but he also taught with conviction and passion.

And second, while Jesus' model of gentle strength applies to both men and women, it's even more important for us to master because of our culture's (including our church culture's) expectations for women leaders. People expect us to overemphasize our gentleness and be wimpy. Or they expect our pendulum to swing the other direction so we overemphasize our strength and become witches (or some other word that rhymes with that). While it's tempting to succumb to cultural expectations, ask God to help you figure out how to be a leader of gentle strength.

Wear Blinders

Is it just me, or do women in youth ministry care more about what others think of them than their male counterparts do? We seem to be far more worried about what parents will think about our sex-ed series, what our pastor will think about our new bongo-drum-led worship music, and what the youth staff will think if we cancel the staff Christmas party. In many ways, that sensitivity to people's feelings is helpful. But in others, it's harmful. It causes us to doubt ourselves and hesitate before we pull the trigger. Instead of "Ready, aim, fire!" we women are more like "Ready, aim, aim, aim, aim, aim...fire?" And even when we do fire off some changes, we still lie in bed at night wondering how others will respond.

Another term for this is (get ready...) People Pleaser. Shamefully, I've fallen victim to this more times than I can count. I often feel the pressure to perform. To be the best at everything, not failing at anything. You know the feeling...to be everyone else but you for the sake of being liked.

It took me a year to finally realize that God didn't bring me to Saddleback in order to be the "guy next to me." He brought me there to bring my unique giftedness to a place that desperately needed it. It needed my energy, my insights, my experience, and yes, even my sensitivity to help not only students grow, but our team as well. Don't doubt your unique giftedness; rather, have a teachable spirit while trusting yourself.

—*Megan*

If this is you, you need some blinders. Don't let the static of others' opinions block your divine antennae. Figure out what God wants you to do and then do it. Along the way, invite people on board the vision, but don't get stalled at the station of What If People Don't Like It?

Bragging Using Christian-ese

"Oh, God is doing *so much* in our ministry. Our small groups are doing great, and TONS of kids are becoming Christians." It's tempting to speak about all the things "God is doing" as a cover for our own bragging. When you share about your ministry, are you really trying to give God the glory or would you like a few crumbs of that glory for yourself? If it's more about you than God, then maybe you should stop sharing for a while. Silence may just turn your character golden.

The Christian "F Word"

You've probably heard the Christian "F Word" bounce its way around your church lobby. It's four letters long. You know what I'm talking about—*fine*.

"How are you?"

"*Fine*, how are you?"

"How are your kids?"

"Oh, just *fine*."

"How's work going?"

"*Fine*, thank you."

When I say I'm "fine," I'm taking the easy way out: figuring out the quickest response that protects me from sharing how I'm really doing.

So I'm on a personal crusade to abolish the word *fine*. When are we ever just fine? I bounce around from denial to despair, hardly ever landing at absolutely fine. Saying "I'm fine" is a cop-out.

What words do you use to cover up how you're really doing? When we combine our insecurities with our No Time To Really Hear How You're Doing culture, we end up with the perfect formula for superficiality. Please, by God's grace, open yourself up to others. Share how you're really doing, what you're really struggling with. Use words like *fantastic, miserable, ecstatic, hopeless.* Let your friends and your students peer into the full range of your emotions.

As I have battled between feeling the need to be strong and wanting to be honest and truthful, I have found a way to be victorious. The question usually comes when I'm having a day like no other—you know the kind: I run out of deodorant (and the last of it actually shoots out of the container all over the black shirt I had laid out to wear!), the car doesn't start in the cold Minnesota morning, I walk into the church building fully aware that I wouldn't be walking out for another 16 hours, and the first voice mail I listen to is from a seventh grader's mom asking, "Will you have any other chaperones with you when you take the 100 junior highers to the Mall of America on Friday?"

And then comes the question as I walk toward the resource room—"How are you doing?" Do I lie and say that life has never been better? Do I look straight at the custodian, who just asked me this seemingly harmless question, and say, "Sit down, and I'll tell ya!" Well, both responses would cause some pain. First, pain for me as I hide the frustration of the day. Second, pain for the friendly custodian who finds out way more than he wanted to know about me.

Instead I have learned to say, "Thanks for asking. I'm actually having a rough day, but I'm looking forward to it getting better!" If the person tries to dig deeper, and I'm not ready to share, I say, "Thanks for caring, but I'd prefer not to talk about it right now." It may sound simple. It may even sound a bit short. But it is a beautiful mixture of humanity and truth that draws a distinctive boundary in your ministry.

—Heather

Mall Rats

What's an easy activity to do with teenage girls? Go to the mall. And when you go to the mall, how do you end up feeling about yourself? Usually worse. You don't have the right body to fit into the clothes—and even if you did, you don't have the money to buy them.

Come up with some other activities to do with girls. Bake dinner together, volunteer to baby-sit for a single parent at your church, or make posters for the next overnighter. And when you do take them to the mall, use it as a springboard for discussion about body image, materialism, and consumerism (and any other isms you can think of).

"Look, Up in the Sky! Is It a Bird? Is It a Plane?"

No, it's Super Woman in Youth Ministry, who, disguised as (fill in the blank with your own name), fights a never-ending battle for salvation, sanctification, and the youth-group way!

Are you tempted to try to do it all? Do your insecurities motivate you to pretend you're the perfect youth worker? If so, then you're only a few steps shy of fatigue and stress. And after you trip down that road of fatigue and stress for a while, you'll stumble into burnout. Instead of caring too much, you won't care at all.

Exit quickly by admitting your weaknesses—both to yourself and to others. Don't try to do it all. Ask others for help. Instead of putting up a façade of having it all together, let others know about your failures and weaknesses. Start with baby steps, like sharing an illustration in a talk about an issue you're struggling with. The phrase "be real" is so overused that we've grown numb to the power of its message, but still: Be Real.

> **As Archibald Hart** from Fuller Theological Seminary explains, "Stress may kill you prematurely, and you won't have enough time to finish what you started. Burnout may never kill you, but your long life may not seem worth living."[5]

Damsel in Distress

Maybe you're on the other end of the spectrum from being a Super Woman. You're more of a damsel in distress: downplaying your own abilities, quickly admitting your flaws, and just waiting for someone (especially a guy) to help you. As the theologian Jurgen Moltmann warns,

> It is usually said that sin in its original form is man's wanting to be as God. But that is only the one side of sin. The other side of such pride is hopelessness, resignation, inertia, and melancholy...Temptation then consists not so much in the titanic desire to be as God, but in weakness, timidity, weariness, and not wanting to be what God requires of us.

While interviewing for jobs, women tend to attribute their past success to luck, or a mentor's help. In contrast, men tend to associate their success with their own abilities.[6]

If this is you, then it's time to recognize that when God calls, he always equips and provides. And while that often happens through others, that's no excuse to avoid stepping up to the plate and taking a swing every once in a while. The next time someone is leading a crowdbreaker involving eggs, ketchup, and pantyhose, raise your hand to play. On the next winter retreat, rally the girls and women in your group to carry their own luggage. Instead of insisting, "Oh, I could never speak in front of our students," volunteer to lead at least a short devotional. Your girls are watching your every move, and you want them to have enough internal strength so they won't need to read books like *Why Do I Think I Am Nothing without a Man?* After all, there is no counterpart for male readers called *Why Do I Think I Am Nothing without a Woman?*

Emotional Affairs[7]

You're partnering in youth ministry with great guys, you're seeing lives changed, and you're passionate about ministry. You may not realize it, but it's easy to let that passion spill over into unhealthy relationships with your male volunteers or paid coworkers. Odds are good—not great, but good—that you're sidestepping the more obvious landmines of inappropriate physical intimacy. However, you might be injured by a more common youth worker trap: inappropriate emotional intimacy.

No one ever talks about this in Christian colleges or seminaries. And I rarely hear about it in training conferences. But across denominations, men and women are having emotional affairs. They're staying out of bed, but they're letting their emotions run wild. They're not abandoning their families, but their coworkers have become pseudo-spouses. Here are some signs you might be in trouble:

- Your coworker becomes your best friend. When you get good news, he's the first person you e-mail. When you get bad news, he's the first person you page.

- You intentionally schedule your hours of ministry to overlap with his, even when you're not meeting together. You'd much rather be around the office if he's there too, even if it means juggling your schedule to do it.

- You find yourself scheduling more time alone with him. Whether you're planning the winter calendar or developing a recruiting strategy, you don't invite others to join you. You like the dynamic better when it's just the two of you.

- You're somewhat jealous of his other female friends. It's not that you don't want him to date or have other friends. You just don't want it to interfere with your time together or the depth of your sharing.

- You actually find yourself jealous of the 13-year-old girls he's talking to. You look across the room and wish you were the one he was comforting or teasing instead of her.

- You start losing sight of his other relationships. He may be married or dating, but you start forgetting about that part of his life. You'd rather just think of him as your partner.

- You choose time with him ahead of your own family or significant friends. After Wednesday night youth group, you head out to coffee with him instead of curling up in front of the fire with your husband. And even if you discipline yourself to head home to your family, in your heart of hearts, you'd rather be out with him.

- You find yourself thinking about him even when you're not with him. You wonder what he's doing and maybe even call him just to say "Hi."

If there's any flavor of inappropriate emotional intimacy in your relationships, talk to a trusted friend about it. Get to know his wife or girlfriend. Reduce the time you're alone with him. Take steps now to put on the brakes before you end up speeding out of control.

> **In three different surveys**, 10 to 12 percent of Protestant pastors have confessed to having extramarital sexual intercourse since they entered the ministry.[8] When the question is broadened, somewhere between 23 percent and 39 percent of pastors admit to having engaged in inappropriate sexual behaviors beyond just intercourse.[9] Approximately 70 percent of these sexual behaviors occurred with someone from the pastor's own church, either a congregation member or a coworker.[10] Like a tidal wave, acts of sexual misconduct by Protestant and Roman Catholic clergy are sweeping away gifted, and probably called, men and women.

Accountability

We've bumped up against the idea of accountability relationships already in this section, but it's so important that it deserves its own tip. By accountability, we mean inviting others to speak into your lives. And whether you're a rookie or a veteran woman in youth ministry, you need other women who love you too much to let you get away with stuff.

Ask one to three women to meet with you regularly. When you meet, covenant together for total honesty and total confidentiality. As you get to know each other, try asking some of the following questions:

- How has your relationship with Christ been changing?
- What's going on in your prayer life?
- How have you encountered God's Word recently?
- How have you served other people this week?

- How have you been treating your family?
- What was your biggest disappointment? How did you decide to handle it?
- What was your biggest joy? How did you handle it?
- How have you been tempted recently? How did you respond?
- How have you controlled your tongue?
- Have you committed any sexual sin?
- How have you worshiped God recently?
- How are you letting non-Christians know about your faith?
- What are you wrestling with in your thought life?
- What do you see as your number-one need for next week?
- Have you lied in your answers to any of the above questions?

Years ago in therapy, I learned two major themes that have saved me time and time again:
- Be true to yourself
- Stay centered

Now I realize this may sound a little psycho-babbleish, but hang with me a second. "Be true to yourself" means being true to what God created you to be—nothing more, nothing less. "Staying centered" means trusting your gut, which is where the Holy Spirit dwells. So whenever I feel like I'm going to lose myself, I'll pause, take a deep breath, and remind my heart and soul: *be true to yourself and stay centered.* This is the essence of knowing whose I am—a treasured child of the King!

—*Megan*

For me, this happens every other Thursday as I meet with a handful of close women friends. No husbands, no kids, no distractions. Each of us takes about 20 minutes to share a few areas in our lives where we need advice, prayer, or accountability. Anyone can ask any follow-up question. Every once in a while there are tears, usually there is laughter, always there is honesty. Thanks to these women, I'm a better follower of Christ, wife, mom, minister, friend, and coworker.

Whose Are You?

I saved the best for last—*Who you are comes out of whose you are.* Memorize this. Meditate on it. May it be your rock in a sea of stress and struggles.

Notes

[1] Allison Pearson, *I Don't Know How She Does It* (New York: Alfred A. Knopf, 2002)

[2] Tim Hansel, *When I Relax I Feel Guilty* (Elgin, Illinois: David C. Cook Publishing, 1979), 37.

[3] Eugene Peterson, *Working the Angles* (Grand Rapids: Eerdmans Publishing, 1987), 52.

[4] Merton Strommen, Karen E. Jones, Dave Rahn, *Youth Ministry That Transforms* (Grand Rapids: Zondervan, 2001).

[5] Archibald Hart, "Understanding Burnout," *Theology, News and Notes* 31, no. 1 (March 1984): 5.

[6] Don Oldenburg, "When Women Play Down Achievements," *Los Angeles Times*, 13 May 1992, sec. E2

[7] This section and sidebar were adapted from Kara Powell's article "Mars and Venus: Too Close for Comfort?" *Youthworker* journal 19, no. 3 (2003): 28–31.

[8] Richard Blackmon, "The Hazards of the Ministry" (Ph.D. diss., Fuller Theological Seminary, 1984); T. Muck, "How Common Is Pastoral Indiscretion?" *Leadership* 9, no. 1 (1988): 12; Baptist Press Archives, April 19, 1996.

[9] Blackmon; Muck, 12–13.

[10] Muck, 12–13.

YOUR
RELATIONSHIPS

YOUR RELATIONSHIPS

The Obi-Wan Kenobi Principle: Mentoring

Growing up, my mom let me have my very own Christmas tree in my very own bedroom. Her one rule: I could only dress the tree with homemade decorations. I summoned all of my eight-year-old creativity to wad up tinfoil and to glue yarn to pieces of cardboard to make the ornaments. I formed a star for the top with bent pipe cleaners, Popsicle sticks, and a gallon of Elmer's glue. The final touch was red and green construction paper loops that formed a chain of garland and covered the tree from tip to trunk. It was really the red-and-green chain that brought life to the tree. Without that chain, the tinfoil and Popsicle sticks would have looked pretty pathetic.

In the history of Christendom, it has been the chain of faith that has brought life to our tradition. The chain is formed by heroes of the past, strugglers of the present, and leaders of the future who pass truths—wrapped up in their own experiences—down the line to the next follower. The sparkly tinfoil of church fads somehow falls aside, but the tradition of passing down the faith—from individual to individual and from community to community—doesn't end.

You are part of that chain. And so are the students you love. In this section, we're going to discuss how to pass down our heritage and love for Jesus through mentoring relationships. When you mentor someone, you empower them. May you not only have mature folks empowering you, but may you also pass what you've learned down to the next generation.

The word _mentor_ comes from _The Odyssey_, which was written by the Greek poet Homer. As Odysseus prepared to fight in the Trojan War, he realized he was leaving behind his one and only son and heir, Telemachus. Since "Telie," as he was known, was a young adolescent (think junior higher), and since wars tended to drag on for years, Odysseus recognized that Telie needed someone to teach him how to be a king while Odysseus was off fighting battles. He hired a trusted family friend to be Telie's tutor. And do you know the name of that trusted family friend? You guessed it—_Mentor_.

It Takes a Village

Many women in youth ministry think a "mentor" is a perfect guru who can spend two to three hours per week with her protégé, coaching her in everything from how not to get ripped off by auto mechanics to how to have a more intimate prayer life. Most of us don't have someone like that in our lives. And when it comes to youth ministry, since many of us don't have the time to really do that—and we certainly can't do that for more than one student—we walk around feeling guilty for all we're NOT doing.

We need a new picture of mentoring. You've heard the African proverb popularized by the Former First Lady, Senator Hillary Clinton: "It takes a village to raise a child." (Maybe you've also heard the tongue-in-cheek version: "It takes a village to raise an idiot.") The same is true with mentoring. There is probably a whole host of people who are currently empowering you. In the same way, you should view yourself as part of a large web of folks God uses to impact students. The results? You take yourself less seriously, you feel more freedom to have unique mentoring relationships with each student, and you're more grateful for the people pouring into you.

Different Strokes

There is no one-size-fits-all mentor. Instead there are different types of mentors, each with their own, unique empowering purpose.

- The most intense form of mentoring is discipleship. A discipler is highly committed to you and teaches you the basics of following Christ.

- A less intense form is a spiritual guide or spiritual director. This person helps you make the decisions that are key to spiritual maturity.

- A third type of mentor is a coach. As in athletics, a coach provides the motivation, skills, and application required to meet a specific task.

- A sponsor is someone who shares the contacts, career guidance, and protection needed to move within an organization or arena.

- The final and least intense form is a model. A model provides an example that inspires and teaches.

As you are both receiving and giving mentoring, identify what kind of relationship you have. Talk about it openly with the other person(s) involved. That way, you'll have clear expectations and no one will expect too much or invest too little.[11]

Put It in Writing

Yesterday a woman in youth ministry approached me, "Kara, I know you're really busy, but I'm wondering if you could maybe mentor me." I told her what I tell every person who asks me that question: Please write down the areas in which you want to be mentored.

There are many advantages to asking people to be more specific about the kind of help they want from you. First, it helps them to think through their expectations for your relationship. Second, it lets you figure out whether you have the experience and expertise that matches their needs. When women or girls ask me to mentor them, at least 50 percent of the time what they really want is counseling, not mentoring. While I know a bit about counseling, I'm no expert. But I know people who are. So I'll meet with them a few times and then give them a few phone numbers of qualified, inexpensive counselors in our area for ongoing follow-up. That way I get them the help they really need.

R-E-S-P-E-C-T

I believe it is impossible to have a true relationship with someone if you don't respect them. The same is true with mentoring—it won't happen without attraction, and attraction is based in respect. Before you ask someone to mentor you, or agree to mentor someone else, make sure you can think of at least one thing you respect about that person.

Bring With

Rarely go anywhere alone. Bring along the people you're mentoring. From buying supplies for Sunday's crowdbreaker to grocery shopping, the extra 15 minutes it takes to pick up or drop off a few students is worth it. They'll remember the conversation you had as you walked down the aisle of a grocery store far longer than they'll remember even your wittiest talk in front of the youth group.

> **One of my favorite parts** of my ministry is attending the events of my kids! There's nothing like the eighth-grade rendition of *West Side Story* or a color guard competition to remind me why I love junior highers! Recently, I've started to invite other kids from that same school or neighborhood to accompany me to the event. If the performing student and watching student are already friends, it brings great happiness to both. If they're not yet friends, I often see a relationship start within weeks of the event!
>
> *—Heather*

Dive In

In mentoring relationships there is a "swimming pool of vulnerability." The person you're mentoring will rarely go deeper than you do. When you stay three-feet deep, so will they. But when you go nine-feet deep, they'll take a deep gulp of air and dive in with you.

Accentuate the Positive

If you're mentoring someone in a particular task (like giving talks at your youth ministry), then make sure you accentuate the positive. It's just as important for people to know what they're doing *right*, so they can repeat it, as it is for them to know what they're doing wrong. For example, after Jane gives her talk, ask: "What do *you* think you did well?" After she has shared, add some things that you think she did well. Then ask: "What do you think you should do differently next time?" Again, after she has told you what she didn't do well, then you add your own opinions. Not only have you accentuated the positive, but you're also giving the person skills to evaluate themselves for a lifetime.

Dear Abby Missed the Point

If you're taking your mentoring cues from Dear Abby, you're missing the point. The "Dear Abby" column is full of answers, but it doesn't ask enough questions. When someone in your ministry asks for help, listen carefully, ask some questions, and then listen some more. Ideally, you should use questions to help that person figure out his or her own answers. Questions like:

- What do you think your options are?
- What do you think you should do? Then follow up with: What do you have to gain from doing that? What do you have to lose?
- Think of someone you respect. What do you think they would tell you to do?
- What would you tell someone else in your situation?

If, after going through several cycles of listening and asking questions, you think the student is still headed down the wrong path, then you owe it to them to speak up with your own advice.

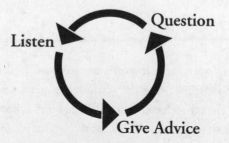

Listen → Question → Give Advice

My college mentor, Sherry, used to say to me, "Heather, no matter how one-sided a disagreement may appear, each person is contributing something to the tension." So often kids go on and on about how awful and cruel their parents are—too strict, never pay attention to me, won't let me date, hate all my friends, and so on. After listening and asking questions, I'm sure to ask, "Kelly, I can see how this is frustrating to you; but tell me, are you contributing to the tension?" After inspecting the carpet for a moment, Kelly usually confesses to slamming doors, sneaking out, throwing tantrums, and ignoring chores. Now we're getting somewhere!

—*Heather*

Make It Mutual

When you're mentoring someone, try to figure out something you can learn from them. One of the eighth graders I am currently mentoring is one of my evangelism heroes. She invites more people to dedicate their lives to Christ by accident than I do on purpose. Sure, I'm older and can help her in all sorts of areas from getting along better with her step-dad to what to do when someone offers her alcohol. But as a woman in youth ministry, I believe God places others in our lives to sharpen us and teach us how to love him more, whether they are 14 or 44 years old.

Just Between You and Me

Whether you're the mentor or the one being mentored, make sure everyone involved agrees to keep quiet about what is discussed. And that includes sharing prayer requests that only serve to "pray someone in the back."

A High Bar

Here's a shocking statement: If someone wants to molest children or teens, there's no better way for the molester to get access to them than through a church. Think about how lax we've become about protecting the kids in our ministry. Youth ministries are so hungry for volunteers that if someone wants to join our team, all they do is meet with the youth pastor and fill out an application. Ten days later we entrust them to drive kids around, counsel them at restaurants, and maybe even have a slumber party with them.

I'm all for relational ministry—I've got eight girls coming to my house for pizza tonight. And I want the other leaders and mentors in our ministry to hang out with kids as well. But in order to protect your students, make sure you do the following:

1. When someone is applying to be a volunteer in your ministry, ask for references. Contact two to three people who know them well and ask: What would make this person a good mentor or leader? What concerns would you have about this person serving as a leader in a youth ministry? What else do I need to know about them?

2. Approach your church about investing the time and money required to work with local police agencies and use fingerprinting as part of your screening process.

3. Teach your mentors and leaders that they should avoid going anywhere alone with a kid—even a kid of the same sex. Try to have another student or leader present in your car or at the coffee house. If you need to talk one-on-one with a kid, make sure their parents know about it and do it in a public place. Even our most innocent intentions can be misunderstood by teens or their families.

When trying to implement a policy like this, sometimes we worry about how a parent may be inconvenienced or upset at having to drive their child to meet us. Before asking the parent, remind yourself WHY the policy is in place—for the protection of the child (and you!)—and communicate that same reasoning to the parent when setting up the one-on-one. I find that 98 percent of the time, parents are so incredibly thankful that we care that much about their kid, they are delighted to drive him or her anywhere!

—*Heather*

A Book Is Worth a Thousand Words

If someone asks me to mentor them and I don't have the time, I ask them to name some areas of their life where they'd like to experience growth. Then I try to suggest a few magazine articles or books that could help them in those areas. After they've finished reading, we try to meet so I can help them process and apply what they've learned. Thanks to their time spent completing the reading assignment, they get deeper insights, and I get more time with my family.

R.I.P.

Some of my favorite mentors are dead. I've never even met them, but their biographies and autobiographies have changed my life. The next time you want to read a good book, choose one written about Henrietta Mears, Hudson Taylor, Dawson Trotman, or Watchman Nee. While you will never meet them face-to-face, your soul will never be the same.

Should We Stay or Should We Go Now?

Every few months, evaluate your mentoring relationship. Ask the following sorts of questions: Where does this relationship need to head? Given this, what are we doing well? What needs to change? If you can't come up with good answers to those questions, then maybe it's time to stop meeting together. Both of you probably have better things to do with your time.

Why Tom Hanks Needed Wilson the Volleyball: Networking

Networking. It's quite the buzzword—both in secular and Christian circles. But what does it really mean? Simply put, it means coming together to do what we could not do ourselves.

It's easy to feel isolated when you're the only one in the room wearing a skirt. And whether you're a volunteer or a professional, you've probably felt a little "different" from the men around you (and even some of the women!). One of the greatest advantages of networking is that it reminds us we're not alone. You need to network with at least one other woman who can remember the lyrics to the song in your heart—and sing that song to you when your memory fails.

Our Southern California Women's Youth Network (WYN) has been meeting every two or three months since 1996. The mission for our WYN is threefold: to encourage, to equip, and to connect with one another. We draw women, as well as a few men, from San Diego to Visalia (which, if you're not familiar with California geography, is about a 300-mile spread). It's always great to have the men there. I'm not sure if they're there to spy on our secret deliberations, to pick up women, or what; but hey, they get exposed to some of the needs and concerns of women in ministry.

Because of the growing interest, we've divided our Southern California Network into three smaller regions: San Diego, North San Diego, and Orange County/Los Angeles. The regions meet four to six times a year and have anywhere from 10 to 30 folks in attendance at their meetings.

We often gather all three southern California networks together for an annual one-day conference for women in ministry and high school girls. Those events usually draw 300 to 400 women and girls, all eager to be encouraged, equipped, and connected. To find out more, check out www.womensyouthnetwork.org.

Burned Out

Don't fool yourself. You can't do it alone. Check out this story and—even though it's about a man—it will speak volumes to you, too.

A member of a thriving church, who had been attending services regularly, suddenly stopped going. After a few weeks, the pastor decided to pay the man a visit. The pastor found the man at home alone, sitting before a blazing fire, trying to beat back the chill of the evening. Guessing the reason for his pastor's visit, the man welcomed him and led him to a comfortable chair near the fireplace.

The pastor made himself at home but said nothing. In the grave silence, he stared at the dancing flames and burning logs. After some minutes, the pastor took the fire tongs, carefully picked up a brightly burning ember and placed it to one side of the hearth all alone. Then he sat back in his chair, still silent.

The host watched all this in quiet contemplation. As the lone ember's flame flickered and diminished, there was a momentary glow and then its fire was no more. Soon it was cold and dead. Neither man had spoken since the initial greeting. The pastor glanced at his watch and, realizing it was time to leave, slowly stood up, picked up the cold dead ember, and placed it back in the middle of the fire.

Immediately it began to glow once more with the light and warmth of the burning coals around it. As the pastor reached the door to leave, his host said with a tear running down his cheek, "Thank you so much for your visit and especially for the fiery sermon. I shall be back in church next Sunday."

Twenty Minutes Makes All the Difference

One of the best ways our ministry networks its women together (and men, too) is to meet in a room adjacent to our youth room for 20 minutes before our Sunday and Wednesday services start. The purpose of the meeting is sharing and prayer. We share what's going on in our own lives, or in the lives of our students, and then pray for each other. Those 20-minute meetings have become the glue in our staff community, allowing us to pray for people looking for jobs, struggling with their own kids, or dreading going back home for Christmas. We make sure we have at least one adult in our youth room to greet students and to make sure our junior highers don't break anything while we're off praying.

Who's Your Sister?

Who's that woman in youth ministry that you've put on your one-day-when-I-have-time-I'll-call-her-so-we-can-grab-coffee list? You know the one I'm talking about. That woman you respect and who seems like too much fun. Today is the day to call her up and pick a time to meet. Networking starts small, and it starts now.

> **I met Marla** at one of our volunteer staff meetings and from the moment I met her, I knew we'd be Ya-Ya sisters! It started with a walk one (very!) early morning. Now it is a weekly hang time of praying for each other, studying Scripture, sharing vulnerably, or laughing our heads off at something that happened that week. Months before, I began praying for a "sister/mentor," and she was it.
>
> Yes, she's older than me, but you know what? I DIG that! She is a mother of two grown children; I am due with our first. She has lived in the same house for 25 years; we just bought our first. She is incredibly disciplined; I pray for self-control! We're just two women in youth ministry—but together we are learning how to hold things loosely, care for our husbands better, and love students to Jesus.
>
> —*Megan*

No Students Allowed

Try scheduling an event just for the women volunteers in your ministry. No students allowed. Grab coffee after your midweek service or lunch after church on Sunday. Get to know each other as *women*, not just as youth workers. Not only will you benefit, but so will your ministry. Instead of just hearing about the Acts 2 community in the first century, students will see *real* community in the twenty-first century.

Don't Splash Around in the Shallow End

Whenever you're with another woman in youth ministry, take advantage of it! Don't just talk small talk; talk BIG talk. Ask her what books have helped her lately or what new struggles her girls are dealing with. Ask meaningful questions, listen, and then ask some more.

Prayer Partners

Ask the women in your youth ministry to write their name and a prayer request on an index card every few weeks. Next, have them exchange cards with another woman. Invite them to post that prayer card in a place where they'll see it regularly, like on a car dashboard or a bathroom mirror. Not only will the women in your ministry start to get involved in each other's lives, but they'll see how God gets involved, too.

Staff Pals

Do you remember when you started in youth ministry? You probably felt what most women feel: a mixture of "I'm So Excited" (to quote the Pointer Sisters) and "Should I Stay or Should I Go Now?" (to quote the Clash). That's exactly how women feel when they walk into your youth ministry for the first time. Help them step over their fears and into real ministry faster by assigning them a staff pal. Pair every new woman with a more mature volunteer who can introduce her to students, sit next to her as she's learning the ropes, and answer any questions she has. A better entry into your ministry will shorten the learning curve by several weeks and hopefully lengthen the amount of time that volunteer stays with your ministry.

Cast a Wide Net

What other women do you know who care about students at your church?

What other churches do you know in your area? Start keeping a list of women who share a passion for hanging out with sixteen year olds over fruit smoothies. It will come in handy if you ever want to pull them all together.

Men—Can't Live with Them...Can't Live without Them

Lots of men in youth ministry want to empower and support their female coworkers and volunteers. They just don't know how. That's where you come in. Call them and see if they'd like to invite the women in their ministries to a meeting with your growing list of women in youth ministry.

To find out more about other churches, youth workers, or networks in your area, check out www.youthworkers.net or call the National Network of Youth Ministries at 858-451-1111.

Offer Meetings Worth the Time and the Drive

Let's face it—the last thing any of us needs is another meeting. Whether you're meeting with two women at Denny's or 15 women in your youth room, offer meetings that are worth the time. Start by giving women a chance to get to know each other through a few share questions.

Spend the next 30 to 45 minutes in some kind of killer training. The best training topics are those that intersect with women's personal lives as well as their ministry lives. Find the person (male or female) who is best qualified, lives locally, and is available to lead discussions on the following sorts of issues:

- Counseling girls
- Teaching and speaking
- Small group ideas

- Mentoring
- Prayer in the life of a youth worker
- Training other leaders
- Developmental needs of teens
- Youth Culture
- Integrity
- Male/female partnership
- Spiritual gifts
- Campus ministry

Set aside the last 15 minutes for prayer. Women love to huddle together to share personal or ministry burdens.

Notes

[11] Adapted from *Connecting* by Paul D. Stanley and J. Robert Clinton (Colorado Springs: NavPress, 1992).

YOUR MINISTRY

YOUR MINISTRY

Speaking Up as a Woman in Youth Ministry

"Typical woman speaker."

"What do you mean?" I asked my friend, Christopher. We had just heard a woman speak to 400 teenagers about the importance of prayer, and his remark intrigued me.

"Well," he continued, "her voice was whiny, she apologized too much, and she wasn't very funny."

While I disagree with Christopher's stereotypes, I have heard them many times. I've often asked myself: Are there differences in the way men and women communicate? If so, how does that affect our ministries?

After observing hundreds of men and women communicating in large group, small group, and one-on-one settings, I have concluded that there are some differences. But they are not absolute. Rather, they are tendencies. Trends. At this point, it's unclear whether or not these differences are due to our biological nature or our sociological nurture. Either way, we need to identify the differences and see if there is anything we need to change so that the all important kingdom message gets heard.[12]

The Woman in Front of the Crowd

Just Say Yes

When I meet women in youth ministry, they often tell me something like, "I just don't feel comfortable speaking in front of a group. I'm way more comfortable in a small group or one-on-one." There are lots of reasons women in youth ministry should work on getting over their fear of speaking before groups. First, fear is hardly ever a good reason not to do something. Second, the girls (and guys!) in your ministry may never see a woman speaker if you stay silent. Third, you are probably a better speaker than you think. Fourth, if you're looking to get hired at a church or parachurch ministry, most jobs (even part-time jobs and internships) will require you to speak in front of a crowd.

So the next time you get asked to speak at your church or somewhere else, just say "yes." Even if it scares you. Maybe even especially if it scares you. You just never know what God might do.

> **When I enter** public school health classes to teach about abstinence, captivating the audience is essential! Each time, I start by rapidly rattling off random things about me— I've bungee jumped three times, I love country music, I own 103 bottles of nail polish, I have two favorite muscles (and show them, of course!), and I think kissing should be an Olympic sport. Within 60 seconds, each kid has probably found at least one thing to relate to or laugh at. And I'm in!
> —*Heather*

Captivate the Audience

As a rule of thumb, every speaker needs to captivate the audience's interest. Especially female speakers. A typical audience consists of three types of people: those who support female speakers, those who are neutral about female speakers, and those who oppose female speakers. A speaker needs to earn the trust, or at least the respect, of those last two groups of people—and quickly. Unfortunately, people usually decide whether or not they're going to listen to you in the first 60 seconds of your talk. That means your introduction is important.

In my experience, the best introductions are those that tap into the audience's need. Humor is nice, a fun story is a plus, but at the end of the day, an introduction is about connecting with the needs of the audience. You want your audience to think: I have a real need that I don't know how to handle. I need help.

To figure out what to say in your introduction, ask yourself: Why is this talk important to the audience? Once you have an answer, then figure out the best way—a piece of art, a story, a joke, a song, some statistics, a poem, a film clip, or an object lesson—to share it.

> **In my speaking journey**, I've found that a joke can fly with some groups and drop dead with the next. However, humorous stories from my own life, told with confidence and honesty, captivate every kind of audience! Not only does it allow the audience to have a window into my life and personality, but it also allows God to use tougher stuff from my past for his glory!
>
> —Heather

Ha, Ha, Ha!

Do you feel comfortable telling jokes or funny stories in front of a group? If your answer is "not really," then you're part of a large group of Women Who Shy Away from Humor. In a systematic study of joke telling among college students, folklorist Carol Mitchell observed that college men tell most of their jokes to other guys, but they also tell many jokes to mixed groups and to women. In contrast, women tell most of their jokes to other women and very few jokes to groups that include men. Also, men were more likely to tell jokes in a group of four or more people, while women often flatly refused to tell a joke when more than four people were around, instead promising to share the joke later in private.[13]

As a woman in youth ministry, the trick is to discover your own sense of humor. Everyone has one. The key is to find it and fine-tune it. Maybe you're a strong joke teller. Maybe you can tell stories about outrageous uncommon events (à la Kathy Griffin), or stories about typical everyday life (à la Caroline Rhea). Or maybe your humor is more dry and intellectual. Before you stand in front of a crowd, practice telling stories or jokes in small groups. Forced humor is awkward—for you and the students—but natural humor usually wins with a youth audience.

A Mist in the Pulpit

I heard a great saying: "A mist in the pulpit becomes a fog in the pew." Doubly so with a youth audience! If you're misty—unclear—in what you're saying as a speaker, your students will be extra confused. Whether your message is in the form of a story (narrative preaching) or several main points (propositional preaching), can you summarize your main idea in one or two sentences? If not, then maybe your topic is too broad, and you need to spend more time clarifying your big idea.

Wave Your Hands in the Air

In every preaching class I took in seminary, I noticed the women tended to gesture less than the men. When women did gesture, their gestures were small, close to their body, and fairly limp.

Gesture and gesture boldly! Get your whole body involved in what you're saying. Arms, head, legs, hands—your whole body is a communication tool. So use it.

Tape Yourself

The only thing more painful than hearing myself talk on a CD or cassette tape is watching myself on a DVD or videotape. Yet as my gym trainer used to say (to my annoyance), "No pain, no gain." The next time you're speaking, ask someone to record you—either on video or cassette. When you watch or listen to the tape later, you'll learn all sorts of things about how you communicate. Personally, I've learned that I tend to twist the rings on my fingers, lean toward my right, and talk too fast. And the only way I could have learned about these bad habits is by seeing myself on tape.

The Woman in a Small Group

There's No *I* in *Team*

In youth ministry, women have an advantage over men when it comes to working with small groups: We tend to value unity and a sense of teamwork more than men do. This commitment to group cohesiveness starts at a young age.

A study by Marjorie Harness Goodwin reveals that young boys become leaders when they issue orders and get others to comply. In contrast, young girls demonstrate a preference for egalitarian leadership. They begin proposals with words like *let's* and *we* to gain consensus and agreement from the entire group. In addition, when a girl makes a leadership decision, she is much more likely than her male counterpart to explain to the group the reasons for her decision.[14]

This emphasis on teamwork often makes it easier for women to create an atmosphere that is cooperative instead of competitive. The next time you're leading a meeting, ask yourself: What can we do that makes us more of a community than a committee? Even if you're not leading, ask yourself that question and share your ideas privately with the meeting leader beforehand.

As I lead my team of volunteer staff, I always try to find ways to add a fun sense of community to our group. It may be as extreme as loading them all into a 15-passenger van on a holiday like President's Day and taking them three hours away from reality to play, laugh, and eat—or as simple as starting a monthly training meeting by asking, "When you were in junior high, which one of OUR junior highers were you most like?"

—Heather

Silence Isn't Golden

Women tend to interrupt less, contribute less, and share fewer ideas in group discussions then men. Even when women have greater expertise than the men in the group, they are more hesitant to share their ideas.[15] Is it because women have fewer ideas, or is it because we're afraid to share them? I think the latter. I can't tell you how many times I've been chewing on an idea, wondering if I should share it with the group, when someone else (usually a man) shares the very same idea and gets a wildly enthusiastic response.

I make it a personal goal in any meeting, class, or gathering to share at least one thought. It doesn't even have to be all that substantive. When is the retreat going to start? Should we send out a letter about that? How are we going to start the game? But at least I'm making a contribution. I'm getting used to hearing my own voice in the room. And it makes me more ready to speak up the next time I have an even better idea.

Don't Keep Score

On my bad days, I enter meetings with a mental scorecard. How many "good ideas" do I have? Am I in the top 50 percent of contributors in the room, or (gasp, shudder) the bottom 50 percent?

> **"Women who find themselves** unwittingly cast as the listener should practice propelling themselves out of that position...If they have something to say on a subject, they might push themselves to volunteer it. If they are bored with a subject, they can exercise some influence on the conversation and change the topic to something they would rather discuss."[16]
>
> —*Deborah Tannen*

On my good days, I try to picture the group as a community. Every person and every idea is valuable because they each contribute to the process of the community. That lame idea you share might be ignored by most others, but by suggesting a pickle-throwing crowdbreaker, you might trigger a great brainstorm in someone else. Your less-than-helpful idea might be the necessary springboard for true brilliance. That means your contributions are equally important to the final outcome.

Maybe Your Chromosomes Have Nothing to Do with It

Last week I learned something interesting about male/female communication. I was with a group of colleagues (eight male and two female, including me!), and we were debating the best way to phrase our objectives for meeting together. The other woman (we'll call her "Robyn") expressed some uneasiness about the wording of one of our objectives. I wasn't quite sure what she meant, and apparently neither was the rest of the group. Someone else raised his hand to voice a suggestion and we ended up talking about his idea instead.

Yet I was still curious about what Robyn was trying to say. Just as I was about to ask her, "Robyn, I don't think I quite got what you meant before. Can you please explain it again?" someone sitting next to her (we'll call him "Phil") offered a critique of one of our objectives. The rest of the group, including me, nodded as Phil made his suggestion. It was one of the best ideas in the last 30 minutes. I even said something like, "That's a great idea."

The only person who didn't agree with Phil's brilliance was Robyn. She muttered under her breath, "That's what I said before. Why do only men get heard around here?"

Robyn's gender had nothing to do with whether or not her ideas were embraced. It was her own communication skills that made the difference, not her chromosomes. It is certainly true that—at times—women are "less heard" in our culture than men. But before you throw down the "gender card," ask yourself (and maybe someone else, too) if you're the one with the communication problem.

The Woman One-on-One

Rapport Talk Versus Report Talk

As a rule, men tend to prefer "report talk" in which both people focus on the facts. The goal is to identify the problem and the best solution as quickly as possible.

In contrast, women usually prefer "rapport talk." They talk about problems to discuss them, not necessarily to solve them. Often they don't want resolution; they want a listening ear.[17]

As a youth worker, we need a healthy dose of both. All ministry boils down to relationships, so rapport talk is essential. Yet at times, we have to delve into the facts with students and help them make the best decisions.

Ask yourself this question: Right now, what dominates my one-on-one conversations—report talk or rapport talk? Now ask yourself: Which do I need to do more often? Remember your answers the next time you meet with someone.

> **If I am honest**, most of my conversations tend to lean toward rapport talk—a tendency that works well in the junior high world. But I want my students to be balanced in their relationships and communication. So at the end of a deep rapport talk, I ask, "Knowing all that you shared with me, what can I do for you in the next week?" It forces students to think beyond the feelings and allows me to walk away with a tangible objective.
>
> *—Heather*

Women and Conflict

Women in youth ministry often avoid conflict. We want to be "nice," not "mean." On the flip side, sometimes others don't want to confront us about something because they don't want to make us cry.

Neither approach is helpful—or biblical. Avoiding conflict is avoiding part of our leadership responsibility. Jesus teaches in

Matthew 18:15, "If your brother sins against you, go and show him his fault, just between the two of you." Paul admonishes us to speak the truth in love in Ephesians 4:15. When you feel like you need to talk to someone, do so, but not in anger. When someone comes to you, try not to be defensive. Listen, ask questions, and then explain your position. Better to be understood than to be loudly or quietly divided.

When Is It Gossip?

I've learned this about gossip: It's not necessarily something you outgrow. The girls in our ministry aren't the only ones who do it—the women do, too.

The girls in my small group often ask me: "When is it gossip?" My best answer: If it's something you wouldn't say if the person you are talking about is in the room, then it's gossip. The same is true for us when we're a decade or two (or three...) older. If we're talking one-on-one with a student or adult, and they start talking about someone else, odds are good that you need to stop them by saying something like, "You know, it feels like we're starting to gossip a little bit." It may be juicy, but it's just not worth it.

> **We must remember** that we are honored to work with girls during this time in their lives. Never again will they face such a tumultuous time developmentally as they do in their adolescent years. We are privileged to come alongside them during this point in their journey! If there is a higher calling—I want to know about it.
>
> —*Megan*

As someone who spends hours with teenage girls each week, I've come to embrace the wisdom of Mary Pipher. In *Reviving Ophelia*, Pipher warns that our society is a "girl-poisoning culture." The messages of media, family, and friends are toxic to girls, contaminating their views of themselves, infecting them with greater self-hatred.

The only antidote is the grace of Jesus Christ. Learned from Scripture and experienced in community, the grace of Christ rescues girls from their cancer-like sin and self-loathing. There is no age limit to this antidote. The struggles and insecurities we deal with as women can only be cured (at least partially) through Jesus' grace. May we love and serve girls in the spirit of C.S. Lewis who described leadership this way: "Think of me as a fellow patient in the same hospital, who having arrived a little earlier, could give some advice."

More Than Fashion Shows and Facials: Creative Programming Ideas for Girls' Ministry

Blast from the Past

A great resource for understanding and loving teenage girls is your own memory. When is the last time you flipped through family photo albums of when you were 14 or looked through your high school yearbook? If you can't remember, it's been too long. Dust off those pictures, drag out those home movies, and flash back to the ups and downs of your own life as a teenager. If you're feeling really brave, invite some of your girls over and let them see your "old fash-ioned" clothes and hairdos.

Displayed in my office and home are photos of me in a variety of situations: prom (with my BIG 80s' hair!); as a child; a family photo taken in the 1970s; my wedding day; and yes, even the dreaded junior high phase. Students love this! It gives them a good glimpse of my story, so when I ask them about theirs, they're not as threatened or timid.

—*Megan*

Philosophy + Context = Ministry

If I could wave a magic wand and help women in youth ministry learn a few things about ministry to girls, I would want us all to focus on two key questions. First, let's think about our philosophy of ministry. What are we trying to accomplish? Why are those goals worth accomplishing?

Second, let's think about our own ministry context. What kinds of students are in our ministry? What are their needs? What resources are available to meet those needs? When we combine our philosophy with our context, we come up with a framework for our ministry.

So when it comes to girls' ministry, ask yourself: What is my philosophy? What is my overall goal or purpose? What values are connected to that goal? Now ask yourself: What are our girls struggling with right now? What people do I know (volunteer staff, parents, church members, community leaders) who can help them?

Once you've come up with some answers, you're ready to design a framework for your ministry. By doing the hard work of defining your philosophy, you've ensured depth. By asking the tough questions about context, you've made sure that your programs are relevant to the girls in your community. It's a good idea to revisit these questions every six months to see if anything has changed. After all, most of our current ministry problems are created by our own past solutions.

Separate But Equal

Is it just me or do teenage girls lose 20 I.Q. points when they're around high school guys? Those who don't get dumber certainly get more giddy and giggly. That's why your ministry needs "girls-only" events. And we don't just mean frilly, lacy teas. We mean top-notch gatherings that inspire your girls to be the women God has called them to be. Here are some of our best ideas:

Auto Mechanic Class
Do your girls know how to check their car's oil and change a tire? Probably not. Give them more car savvy by having them dress in their grubby clothes and show up at your church parking lot for an auto mechanic class. If you can find a female instructor, all the better!

Guy Panels

Your girls are dying to know what guys think, but they just don't feel safe asking them on their own. Give them an opportunity to ask guys what they really think. Put together an all-male discussion panel. Make sure you invite guys who will be honest and consider including a few college guys for a broader perspective. You can even narrow the focus of your panel to a topic like love, sex, and dating. But if you do, make sure to invite married men to sit in on the discussion as well.

Self-Defense Training

In this culture, what girl doesn't need to know how to protect herself? Invite a self-defense teacher to come speak to your girls and let them practice some of their best self-defense karate chops. Or better yet, invite moms, stepmoms, aunts, sisters, and small group leaders, too.

Outer-Beauty Events

I want the girls in our ministry to know they are beautiful—inside and out. I tell them their outer beauty is like frosting on a cake. Ideally, frosting should enhance the flavor of the cake, but too much can ruin it. The same is true about outer beauty. Spending a little bit of time or money on make-up, hairstyles, and clothes will help people see their inner beauty. But if our girls devote too much time, money, or focus on their looks, they won't have enough energy left over for developing their inner beauty.

So periodically I want to help our girls enhance their outer beauty. We'll have seminars on skin care, make-up, exercise, nutrition, hairstyles, and even fashion shows. But when we do, we make sure to do two things: we offer ideas and products that are affordable, and we stress that ultimately what makes a girl most attractive is her personality, character, and love for others.

Maximize Your Closet

Okay, true confession: When I was in high school, I used to write down what I wore to school so I wouldn't duplicate my outfits. (Isn't it ironic that 15 years later my idea of a great weekend involves wearing the same sweats for 48 hours?!) What teenage girl hasn't stood in front of her closet and scanned her clothes looking for The Right Thing to Wear?

To help your girls maximize their wardrobe without spending an extra penny, ask someone who knows something about fashion to conduct "home visits" for a few of your girls and show them how to make the most of the clothing they own. Ask her to help them create new outfit combinations and make good use of the black skirt that seems out of date or those jeans that just don't fit right.

Make sure to videotape what she says, show the tape at a girls-only event, and then invite her to make some general comments about what all the girls can do to enhance the clothes they already have.

Father-Daughter Pitfalls

Many youth ministries schedule frequent father-daughter events—special dances, beach trips, and Saturday breakfasts just for dads and their girls. While these events can be fantastic opportunities for girls who have dads, they can be excruciatingly painful for those who don't.

When I was welcoming dads and daughters at one Saturday father-daughter breakfast, a girl walked up alone. All of her friends were going to the breakfast, and she wanted to come, even though her dad had left their family years ago. She could barely look me in the eye as I welcomed her, and at one point during the breakfast, I saw tears running down her cheeks. We had even announced during the weeks prior to the event that we could pair girls with "dads for the day" if their dads couldn't come. But she decided to brave it on her own. And while I'm proud of her for coming, I felt nauseous the entire morning.

I decided that day that I would never schedule a father-daughter event again. Maybe you disagree with me, which is fine. But if you do, please think through the kinds of girls you have in your ministry. How many of them don't have dads around? Even if they don't come to the event, how will they feel when you make announcements about it or when their friends are talking about it afterwards?

Sadly, the percentage of absentee moms or dads in the home is increasing. Obviously, we must be sensitive to this as we plan our events. We recently had a mother-daughter event where we advertised by saying "For girls only...and their moms, aunts, sisters, small group leader, or friends." This took the pressure off, and we didn't lose students over an event.

—Megan

Superwomen Series

There's no denying that most of the people in the Bible are men. But note we said "most" and not "all." There are some amazing female heroines of the faith. And the girls (and guys!) in your ministry deserve to hear about them. Sometime soon, do a Superwomen Series. Talk about Deborah, Abigail, Esther, Ruth, Mary (there are lots of them in the gospels; just pick one), and Priscilla. And when you talk about them, please don't paint them as one-dimensional, "perfect" leaders. Show your students their three-dimensional ups and downs. That's real life—both B.C. and A.D.

Quick Relationship Builders

The next time you've got 15 minutes while you're watching TV or waiting for your meatloaf to come out of the oven, try these quick relationship builders.

- Prayer Phone Calls: Wake up early, call a few of your girls before they head out the door to school, and ask them how you can pray for their day. Then pray together over the phone.

- Audio Affirmation: Grab a tape recorder and a blank cassette tape, and record a five-minute affirming message for one of your girls. How many times do you think she'll listen to it? If you answer 10, you're guessing way too low.

- Answering Machine Blitz: Lots of times we only call students when we want to invite them to an event or need something from them. Instead, try calling a girl's voice mail or answering machine five times in one day just to say hello, you love them, you've been praying for them, and you hope their day went well.

- Quick Notes: Most of the girls in your youth ministry are so eager to get mail, they'll open envelopes addressed to "resident" and "occupant." Sometime soon, grab some stationery and write a few quick encouragement notes, letting each girl know how much you appreciate them. That three-minute note is the kind of thing your girls will keep posted on their bedroom mirrors or folded on their nightstand for months.

Most of your girls feel like K-Mart in a Nordstrom world.
—*Kara*

- Parent Affirmation: Most of the time when parents hear from teachers at school, it's because their daughter has done something wrong. Make a parent's day by writing a note or calling to tell them what their daughter is doing right.

Often after small group or church, I will walk a student out to the parking lot so I can meet their parent(s). I will shake the parent's hand and totally brag on their son or daughter until the kid turns red! And you know what? It's win-win for everybody. The parents know their teenager is being loved on, the student feels appreciated, and we (as the youth worker) get to keep loving on them!
—*Megan*

Beyond Doctor Laura: Counseling Girls

Normal or Not?

Much of what we do when we talk to girls is let them know that what they're experiencing is normal. Doubt, anxiety, and fear of rejection are all normal parts of the search for identity that beats at the heart of being a teenager. In other words, we normalize what they pathologize.

Yet on the flip side, we may also need to pathologize what girls normalize. While mild bouts of depression are typical for teenage girls, frequent thoughts of suicide are not. While wishing you weighed fewer pounds is a near universal experience, losing 25 pounds in six weeks isn't. Think of any sudden change in the behavior or appearance of one of your girls as a cry for help.

When You're Over Your Head

From eating disorders to sexual addictions, if you spend much time with teenage girls, you'll quickly realize you're in over your head. If you think one of your girls is dealing with a problem that is beyond your ability to help, your best move is to refer her to a local counselor. Try to find someone who's financially affordable (perhaps they're willing to work on a sliding fee scale) and open to meeting with other members of the family as needed.

What to Do About Abuse

When you encounter a girl who has been abused (note how I said "when," not "if"), make sure you avoid common youth worker mistakes by following these tips. (These aren't gender-specific; they also apply when you are caring for guys who have been abused.)

1. Be sure to tell her that while you value her privacy, you might not be able to keep what she shares confidential. Many women in youth ministry make an absolute promise to their girls that they'll keep whatever is told to them confidential. When it comes to abuse, that's impossible. When I sense a girl is getting ready to tell me about being abused, I usually say something

Read this e-mail from a sophomore in our ministry:

"Okay. I know you don't know me, but I really need someone's advice. Okay. About a week ago I cut myself real bad, and I was put in a hospital to get help. Well, when I left after about a week at the hospital I thought I was ready to go home and not cut myself. But now I realize that I still have the urge to cut myself more, but I don't want to tell anyone I know because I feel like if I tell anyone I know that I will have to go back to the hospital. Now I haven't cut myself yet, but I'm afraid that I might, and then I'll have to go back to the hospital. What do you think I should do?"

This is a great example of someone who needs some serious help from a professional counselor. As this student's youth pastor, I can love her, care for her, and speak truth to her—but I am not her therapist. It is my job to help her find the best professional care possible and hold her hand through her pain.

—*Megan*

like, "I so value what you're telling me, and I want to hear more. But just so you know—in order to help you, I might not be able to keep what you've told me secret." Usually by the time a girl is ready to tell me about her abuse, she's so ready to tell someone that she'll keep talking.

2. Tell your supervisor about the abuse. If you're a volunteer, talk to the youth pastor. If you're the youth pastor, talk to the sen-

A great rule of thumb when a student asks, "Promise not to tell?" is to respond with: "I promise, as long as you are not a harm to yourself or others. I say this because I care for you and want what's best for you."

—*Megan*

ior pastor. Hopefully your church has some sort of written policy describing how to respond to abuse situations; but even if it doesn't, you need to bring your supervisor into the loop before you take any more action.

3. Call Child Protection Services. While laws vary from state to state, odds are good that even if you're a volunteer, you're a mandated reporter. If you're not sure, you can call Child Protection Services (or C.P.S.) anonymously, describe your role in your ministry, and explain what occurred to the student. C.P.S. will be able to tell you whether or not it qualifies as abuse and whether or not you need to report it. Keep in mind that even if you're not a reporter, your supervisor probably is, in which case they will need to report it. ALWAYS remember that you are an advocate for children. Even if the abuser has moved away from the student, he or she may still have the opportunity to abuse others. Working with the correct state authorities, you can prevent this.

The American Association of University Women reports that 50 percent of girls experience unwanted sexual touching in school.[18]

Encourage Girls to Step up to the Plate

Many of the girls in your youth ministry have huge reservoirs of leadership potential just waiting to be tapped. All you have to do is look hard at their potential and then ask them to step up to the plate. Which of your girls are natural leaders? Which of your girls could be leaders if someone just encouraged them and gave them an opportunity?

Invite both types of girls to take some risks in your ministry. Ask them to organize your supply closet (that was my very first leadership job as a 15 year old), greet guests, or help you plan your next girls-only event. After all, while we think the best youth workers are also the best ministers, it's not really true. The best youth workers are those who help others be the best ministers.

Getting Paid for This Crazy Thing Called Youth Ministry

According to Patricia Aburdene and John Naisbitt in *Megatrends for Women*, female leaders in our culture have reached "critical mass." And no, we're not talking about our weight.

What is critical mass? For anyone who hasn't brushed up on their physics lately, critical mass is defined as the point at which a process becomes self-sustaining. In geology, it's when a few rocks falling down the hill evolve into a landslide. In *teen-ology*, it's when a new slang word becomes so popular it's now a common part of everyday language (which someday might happen to my made-up word: teen-ology).

As Aburdene and Naisbitt have surveyed the fields of medicine, law, politics, sports, and even religion, they concluded that by now enough women have entered these fields that people are not only accepting women, but they are also starting to assume they should be there working shoulder-to-shoulder with men. While that's fantastic news for female youth pastors, in many churches, in many parts of the country, and in many denominations, people are slower to fully accept women in leadership. Maybe someday our gender won't matter, but that day is still a few years—if not decades—off.[19]

We've come a long way from the words of the famous philosopher, Jean Rousseau, who wrote 200 years ago, "Women's entire education should be planned in relation to men; to please men, to be useful to them, to win their love and respect, to raise them as children, care for them as adults, counsel and console them, make their lives sweet and pleasant. These are women's duties in all ages; these are what they should be taught from childhood on."[20]

So here we're devoting extra time and energy to thinking about how to be the kind of youth pastor whose effectiveness and integrity earns others' respect—regardless of gender.

More Power to You

In *Real Power*, Janet Hagberg suggests a fascinating paradigm for the development of powerful leadership. She believes there are six stages of power. The first three stages focus on external power—or power based on what others think of you. The last three focus on internal power— or power that flows from inside of you. While her conclusions are relevant to both men and women, we'll apply them just to women.

Stage One: Powerlessness
At this stage women often get manipulated and, in turn, gain power over others by manipulating them. Think of Ethel Mertz from *I Love Lucy*— she never came up with any plans on her own; she was a pawn in that outrageous redhead's schemes.

Stage Two: Power by Association
At stage two women gain power by being apprentices, either through official internships or unofficial mentoring. Carol Brady from *The Brady Bunch* is a great example here. Most of her power came only as she echoed her husband's words, "Your father's right, kids…"

Stage Three: Power by Symbols
The key at stage three is control. Power comes through salary, job titles, or name-dropping. A great example is Sydney from the television show *Alias*. She uses her physical power and the resources of "the agency" as the basis for her own strength.

Stage Four: Power by Reflection
At this stage women are transitioning from external power to inner power. This is the beginning of true leadership and deep exploration. C.J. Craig, the press secretary character on *The West Wing*, shows power by reflection—she's not only willing to arrive at her own conclusions, but she also expresses them to other powerful leaders.

Stage Five: Power by Purpose

At stage five women gain a purpose that extends beyond themselves. Oprah Winfrey's commitment to life transformation—for both herself and others—is a classic stage-five approach to leadership.

Stage Six: Power by Gestalt

At the final stage of leadership, women are peaceful, quiet servants who have enormous influence at broad levels. While very few women ever reach this stage, Mother Teresa provides an example of the humble strength that marks this final gestalt.[21]

What stage best characterizes you? What do you think it would take for you to move forward to the next stage? Here are some suggestions:

1. Regularly create some time and space for you to reflect. Make a cup of tea, find a comfy chair, and spend some time journaling or reflecting about who you are and who you are becoming.

2. If you're an extrovert and learn more by talking to others, try asking some people who know you well to answer the same two questions about you: *Who am I?* and *Who am I becoming?*

3. Develop your own life purpose statement. Ask yourself two key questions: *Who do I want to be?* and *What do I want to be?*

4. Ask yourself: How much of my time is consumed by anger or fear? Anger and fear are two of the primary thieves of inner power.

5. Spend time with others who lead with inner power. What can you learn from them?

The Opportunity Pendulum

If you're like me, your experience as a female youth pastor has been a mixture of hills and valleys. At times I have felt so affirmed as a pastor: I have been asked to be involved with certain events because they "needed a woman's perspective." I've been asked to speak at different camps and conferences because no woman had ever spoken there before and some progressive man felt like it was time (or past time) to have a woman speak. I've received job offers because churches and universities are embracing the idea of male/female partnership.

After a two-year journey from the intern, to the associate, to the junior high pastor, I was introduced to a group of senior pastors from local churches as the "Junior High Intern." My heart sank. But as I walked toward the podium to give my presentation, I thought to myself, I know what I do, the kids know what I do, and God knows what I do. That's all I need. That day, instead of being discouraged and annoyed, I presented my information with more passion and clarity than I ever had before.

—*Heather*

But other times it's been tough. Sometimes it's the little things—like people who stop by our student ministry office and assume I'm the secretary because I'm the first woman they see. Or when I went for my daylong interview to be licensed in my denomination and had two male candidates ask me where my husband was, assuming he was the one being licensed and I was just along for the ride. Other times it's the bigger things, like when I came to one church as the first female college pastor and a few students and families left the church before they even met me, simply because of my gender.

Female youth pastors often swing back and forth on the opportunity pendulum. Sometimes opportunities are placed right in front of us because we're female; other times they're kept permanently just beyond our reach. If you're swinging toward the side of great opportunities, keep in mind that each opportunity is a gift from God, not something you "deserved" or "earned." If you're swinging toward the side of few opportunities, remember that God cares more about who you are than what you do. And so do the people who love you the most.

Catch-22

There's a strange Catch-22 for women looking for a job in youth ministry. On the one hand, many women don't know where to look to find job openings. On the other hand, churches and ministries hoping to hire women don't know how to find them.

There are some people and organizations that can help do some matchmaking. First, try your denomination's regional or national headquarters. Odds are good they have a database that lists open positions and people looking for ministry jobs. Second, check out the job bank postings or post your own resume at www.youthspecialties.com. Third, contact the National Network of Youth Ministries at www.youthworkers.net and see if the regional or local coordinator in your community knows of any possibilities.

Behind Door Number One

Whether there are more or fewer leadership opportunities open for you, the critical thing is to find the ONE door—God's door—and walk on in, sister.

To Ordain or Not to Ordain

There are denominations that ordain women, and then there are those that don't. There are those that fall somewhere in between and technically they ordain women, but in reality it only happens once every leap year.

Where does your denomination fall? Find out today and decide if you're comfortable with its position. If not, prayerfully consider whether you should work from within your denomination to bring change, or perhaps search for another denomination in which to serve. Know that if you and the folks in your denomination disagree

Although I grew up and am currently in a denomination that is hesitant to ordain women, I have found a church that values and celebrates women in ministry. I am one of three female pastors on staff and am asked to preach to the overall congregation each year. I can marry couples and perform funerals. My opinion is sought out and heard. For me, it's a great fit, and I am free to follow God's call on my life in this encouraging environment, even without being ordained.

—Heather

about the role of women in leadership, you'll probably be frustrated...and so will they!

Beyond the Church

Parachurch ministries are often more open to women in leadership—in both volunteer and paid positions. If you're hitting a glass ceiling, try a whole new room. Check out Youth for Christ, Young Life, Fellowship of Christian Athletes, Student Venture, and a whole bunch of other quality, parachurch ministries. Never, never, never give up.

> **Women at the highest levels** of business are rare. They comprise only 10 percent of senior managers in Fortune 500 companies.[22]

A Dollar Is a Dollar Except If...

According to a finding from a recent study by the Pulpit & Pew research unit of Duke Divinity School (using data from a national survey of pastors in 2001), "Female clergy on average earn $6,500 less than male clergy, although average household income for female clergy is higher than for male clergy households due to working spouses."[23]

Some women think that as long as their bills are paid, that's fine. They didn't go into ministry for big bucks in the first place. Others think that equal work demands equal pay. Whether or not they have a family and whether or not they are the sole breadwinner is irrelevant.

Both extremes are flawed. On the one hand, you may be setting a dangerous precedent for the women who follow you (women who aren't as keen on Top Ramen and thrift-store shopping as you are). On the other hand, Jesus was more about sacrifice then entitlement.

My best advice is to find out the salary parameters that your church or ministry has set up for its staff. Then instead of asking for the same salary as "Joe" (which makes it personal), ask to be paid according to the established parameters.

The First Decade

In your first decade of ministry, God cares more about what he's doing in you than through you. That's so important—I'm going to say it again: *In your first decade of ministry, God cares more about what he's doing in you than through you.* Actually, that's true for every decade of your ministry, but it's especially true in your first 10 years.

So if you're a rookie, keep asking yourself: *What is God trying to teach me? Even if I'm not seeing much fruit now, how is he trying to form my character to create a lifetime of fruitfulness?* And if you're beyond your first decade, keep that in mind as you talk to younger women who are taking themselves and their ministries a bit too seriously. Refocus them on who they are becoming, not what they are doing.

Be Professional

I wish it weren't this way, but our culture still tends to assume men are the primary leaders. If you're the youth pastor, one way to gain a bit more credibility is through professionalism. When you run meetings, do you show that you value others' time by having a clear purpose and providing a printed agenda? Do you show up for meetings and events on time? Do you give students, families, and your volunteer team a few weeks' notice before scheduling an event? Does the way you dress earn you respect? Or are you dressed so immodestly or so casually that others might not take you seriously at first?

Again, I wish it weren't this way, but female youth pastors need to be more professional than our male colleagues. In some people's eyes, the fact that we're female already puts us in a hole, so we have to do extra work to climb out and stand on equal footing.

> **When I first entered into ministry**, it was through the camping ministry door. My daily attire always included some sort of plaid, cut-off shorts, and flip-flops. I found out quickly that institutional (or church) ministry had a different dress code! After realizing the "unwritten" dress code was not a conspiracy against me and that I could still be who God created me to be—in dress slacks—I understood. You see, I have a switch. It can be flipped in any situation and produce change. When I am at an all-nighter with my kids, my switch empowers "Crazy Heather!" As I walk up front to lead communion for the congregation, the switch empowers "Serious Heather." Both true. Both me. Both professional.
>
> *—Heather*

The Poster Child

One of the difficulties of being a female youth pastor is that you become the poster child for women in youth leadership. Since our male colleagues don't know a lot of female pastors, we become The Voice for All Women in Youth Ministry.

Sometimes I barely even know what I think, let alone what All Women in Youth Ministry think. If the pressure is starting to get to you, speak up. Let those around you know that your opinions are just that—your opinions. If they want to know what women in general think, they can't base their conclusions on just you. Other women need to be integrated into the leadership circle.

All You Can Eat Lobster

According to Janet Hagberg in *Real Power*, women are like lobsters in a pail. Just as one woman starts to make her way out of the pail, other women who want to do likewise yank her hind claws and try to pull themselves out by using her as a ladder. The result? A massive heap of claws and shell fragments are left at the BOTTOM of the pail.

We women can be vicious to each other. We can be judgmental, and we can be jealous. We're often harder on other women than we are on men, especially when we're jealous of them. The next time you have a chance to criticize another woman in youth ministry, keep your mouth shut. Let her inch out of the pail. Or let her stand on your shoulders to get a head start.

The Honorary Man Syndrome

When I first graduated from seminary and started working at a church as a youth pastor, I worked on a pastoral team with seven pastors. Guess how many women were on the pastoral team? One total. Me.

Every Monday we went out to lunch together before our weekly staff meeting. Every Monday I intentionally wore pants. Why? On one level it was because I was tired of being the only one climbing into the backseat of a two-door Honda Civic in a skirt. But on a deeper level, I was tired of being different. I was tired of being the only one wearing a denim wrap-around skirt in a sea of navy and beige Dockers.

Whether you're a volunteer or a professional, it's easy to fall into the "honorary man syndrome." You become an honorary man when you hide the parts of you that are "feminine" from the rest of the world. (Since coming up with a definition of *feminine* would take a whole separate book, we'll let you define it for yourself.) From superficial things, like the way you dress and the words you use, to deeper parts of you, like the way you inherently treat people and the way you set priorities, the adults and kids you work with deserve to see ALL of you. When you hide part of yourself from them, not only are you robbing yourself, but you're also stealing from them. Let your ministry see all of your colors: the masculine blues and greens and the feminine pinks and purples. The best pictures of your life involve the whole color palette.

The One with the Bra

I once worked with a male colleague whose standard line in meetings was, "The one with the bra takes the notes." No joke.

It's tempting to volunteer to be the note taker in the group. Men expect you to, and you've probably gotten pretty good at it. But try being a little slower to volunteer. Just because you're a woman doesn't mean you have to be the secretary.

Handling Anger

As a female youth pastor, it's only natural to get angry when you bump up against obstacles. Sometimes you might channel that anger at others. Other times you probably keep it pent up until it finally explodes. Neither method works very well.

The next time you're angry about how you're being treated as a woman (or anything else, for that matter), figure out what it is exactly that makes you angry. Did someone wrong you? If so, you have the right to be angry. But if not, then maybe it's your own sin or "issues" that are fanning your fury.

Next, figure out the best way to express your anger. That probably means privately talking to the person who has wronged you.

Finally, ask God to help you forgive them. The greater the forgiveness, the greater the freedom. And while it may take time, it will be worth it.

Who's Your Buddy? Who's Your Pal?

As a female youth pastor, spend some energy building relationships with the following people:

1. The person who signs your check.

2. The person who answers your phone.

3. The person who cleans up after you and your ministry.

These three people have enormous power to make your life easy or to make your life difficult. You will not regret treating them well.

80/20

What are your spiritual gifts? Do you know? If not, then round up a spiritual gifts test, evaluate your own experience, and ask others to give you input about what you do well. Once you know the three or four things you do best, spend 80 percent of your time there. Spend the remaining 20 percent in your weak areas, finding other team members who are truly gifted in those areas to shoulder the bulk of the work. Much of being a female youth pastor is about being focused, so concentrate on your strengths and release others to be strong in your weak areas.

More Degrees Than Fahrenheit

You might guess that I, as someone with a Ph.D., am biased regarding education. And you would be right. The driving reason for my graduate degrees has been my sense that it was part of God's call. A nice secondary benefit has been greater respect from both the men and women of my church. If you think God might want you to finish your college degree, aim for a Master's degree, or maybe even go on to pursue doctoral work—do it. You can always quit if it's too much. But at least you will know you tried.

Notes

[12] A large portion of section 3 is based on a chapter Kara Eckmann Powell wrote for *Breaking the Gender Barrier in Youth Ministry*, edited by Diane Elliot and Ginny Olson (Wheaton, Illinois: Victor Books, 1995), pages 33-50.

[13] Deborah Tannen, *You Just Don't Understand: Men and Women in Conversation* (New York: Ballantine Books, 1990), 89-90.

[14] Ibid, 237.

[15] Ibid, 127-129.

[16] Ibid, 148.

[17] Ibid, 77.

[18] Mary Pipher, *Reviving Ophelia* (New York: Ballantine Books, 1994), 69.

[19] Patricia Aburdene and John Naisbitt, *Megatrends for Women* (New York: Villard Books, 1992).

[20] L.G. Smith, "Centuries of Educational Inequities," *Educational Horizons* 60 (1981), 4-10.

[21] Janet Hagberg, *Real Power* (Salem, Wisconsin: Sheffield Publishing Company, 1994)

[22] Debra E. Meyerson and Joyce K. Fletcher, "A Modest Manifesto for Shattering the Glass Ceiling," *Harvard Business Review* 1999, page 127.

[23] Mark Wingfield, "Should free market determine pastors' pay?" *Biblical Recorder,* February 28, 2003. Retrieved August 28, 2003, from:
http://www.biblicalrecorder.org/content/news/2003/2_28_2003/ne2 80203should.shtml

THE MEN YOU WORK WITH

SECTION FOUR

THE MEN YOU WORK WITH

Mars and Venus in the Ministry

I don't know how it got there. Someone must have given it to me. On my shelf rests a book entitled *What Men Know About Women*. When you open up the book, all you see are blank pages. On the flip side, I think of Henry Higgins in *My Fair Lady* asking, "Why can't a woman be more like a man?"

As a woman in youth ministry, I've felt both. At times, I've felt misunderstood, misjudged, and mislabeled by men. Yet in my insecurity, I've often wished I could be more like men—in order to understand them and to fit in.

The popular book *Men Are from Mars, Women Are from Venus* by John Gray implies that men and women come from two different planets. Frankly, I think that's an overstatement. Yes, we are different, but are we really from two different planets? Perhaps two different neighborhoods is a more accurate description. Or at least we hang out in different parts of town. Yet we youth workers have the same Boss, the same divine Mayor. And at the end of the day, that is what matters most.

"Genderalizations"

For the last decade, I've wrestled with the questions: *Are men and women truly different? Or are we merely exaggerating coincidental, occasional differences?* My answers: yes and yes.

Men and women are different. But the differences aren't inevitable. So I've made up my own label: "genderalization." A "genderalization" is a tendency that consistently differentiates male and female attitudes and behaviors. Note I said "consistently" and not "always." It seems to me that if we were really all that different, God would have said different things to each gender in his word.

So before you throw around stereotypical statements about men and women, ask yourself these questions:

1. Is there any actual research confirming these differences or is it just my opinion?

2. If I look at the overall population, how consistent are the differences between men and women?

3. What else besides gender might be causing the differences?

4. If it probably is gender that is causing the differences, how much of that is innately biological and how much is socially conditioned?

5. Can I be more careful with my language, using words like *tend to*, *usually*, and *often*, instead of throwing down blanket statements about either gender? For example, saying that men *tend to* stay on a superficial level longer in conversations is a much softer statement than saying *all men* are superficial. Plus, it's closer to the truth.

One great rule of thumb is to "put yourself in the other person's shoes." Try to respect what they're saying even if it's not necessarily what you agree with or would choose.

WARNING: Great patience and holding your tongue are required.

Why is all this so important? I believe it's impossible to work with someone if you don't respect them. And if we're always comparing men and women, limiting what each gender can become and judging them because they're different from us, we're bound to lose respect for each other.

Don't Worship the Wiring

It bothers me when people use their gender as a scapegoat for their behavior.

- "I can't help getting all emotional and overreacting—I'm a girl."
- "I can't help looking at other girls. That's what guys do."
- "I know we talk about other people behind their backs, but what can you expect from us girls?"
- "You know us guys. We don't share our feelings very well."

Think about Jesus. While he was biologically a male, he demonstrated qualities that we think of as "masculine" and "feminine." He showed his emotions, but he also helped people solve problems. He acted with passion and even anger, but he also listened with compassion. If the behavior or attitude that you blame on your gender is actually sin, then you have no right using your biology as an excuse. Instead, ask God for his grace to take some steps (even baby steps) to become more of the whole person that Jesus longs for you to be.

Who Am I?

Many men tend to define their sense of self through results, especially at work. Many women tend to define their sense of self through feelings and relationships. Which one is better? Neither. God calls us to something higher. And better. Our ultimate sense of self should come from being his beloved child. The rest is just gravy.

As you work with guys who seem too focused on results, try to refocus them on God's unconditional love. Isn't it amazing that God loves us as much on days when we're lying in bed and watching *I Love Lucy* reruns as on days when we accomplish tons for "his kingdom"?

As you work with women who allow others to define how they feel about themselves, try to refocus them on their relationship with God. As long as we put others in control of how we feel about ourselves, we'll always be controlled by them (makes sense, doesn't it?).

I want you to really get this because if you don't, time and time again you'll shrink back from this high calling of being a woman in leadership. So read the following verse and underline the words *your* or *you* every time you see one of them (underline them a lot if you must): "But now, thus says the Lord, YOUR Creator…And He who formed YOU…'Do not fear, for I have redeemed YOU; I have called YOU by name; YOU are Mine!'" (Isaiah 43:1, NASB).

Yep, that's what God says about YOU. He's called YOU. That means your unique, gifted, broken, sinful, wonderful self. Don't you dare shy away from bringing your true self to the table of youth ministry.

—Megan

The Dark Side: Stereotypes, Discrimination, and Obstacles

Cave or Community

When men are upset, they tend to withdraw. Needing time alone, they take a walk, go for a jog, or hop in their car for a drive. It's their cave.

When women are upset, we tend to want community. We want to talk, feel, and then talk some more.

When you get in conflict with a man in your ministry, usually he wants to take off and you want to sit down and "talk it out." He walks away, you chase him down; he starts running, and then you jet after him. Now you're both sprinting—him away from you. Not a very healthy dynamic.

Ahead of time, talk with the men you work with and figure out a good conflict-resolution process. Would it help if you both wrote out what you were feeling and thinking *before* you talked? Would it help if you took an hour to cool down before you stormed into each other's office and said things you'd later regret (and didn't even really mean)? Can you find a compromise that gives the guy a bit of time alone, but then provides an opportunity to each share how you're feeling? It's naive to think our relationships with men are going to be absent of conflict, but it's wise to work out a conflict resolution plan ahead of time.

Why Are Men in My Ministry Intimidated by Me?

As a woman in youth ministry, do you ever feel like you intimidate some guys in your ministry? It's almost like your competence as a youth worker forces them to retreat. That's probably because feeling needed is a motivator for many men. When it seems like you don't need them, they tend to distance themselves from you.

Unfortunately, many women respond by then hiding their abilities and acting weaker than they really are. By doing this, they're keeping themselves from living the life God intends.

There is a better way. As followers of Christ, we do need each other, regardless of gender. You need men, just like you need women, to speak into your life, sharpen you, and empower you to be the

---

As a strong female, I've learned to apply the 24-hour rule. That is, if I have conflict with a colleague, I wait 24 hours before saying anything. When I do this, I will typically have three results:
1) I'm not as emotional and am able to communicate clearly and compassionately,
2) I am the problem and need to seek forgiveness (that's always fun), or
3) It isn't a battle I need to fight—vengeance was God's, not mine.

Whatever the case, just make sure you are committed to honesty, first with yourself, then with others.

—*Megan*

---

woman you want to be. If a man is intimidated by you, let him know specific areas in which you need him. Do you respect his advice about your ministry's purpose statement? Do you need him to help you flesh out your community outreach plan? That way you're not becoming less of yourself, but you're allowing him to be more of himself.

Compliment Men to Others

Regardless of how similar or different you are from the men in your ministry, you have enormous power in shaping what students think of them. If a male staff member drops the ball on something, do you try to help him figure out a good plan B, or do you make sarcastic comments for all to hear? If one of the guys on your team doesn't discipline that overly rowdy senior very well, do you talk to him about it in private, or do you verbally slam him in front of others?

Students are more attentive to our comments about other adults than we think. Are you reinforcing the messages that many (especially girls) hear at home about how worthless men are, or are you giving your students a hopeful picture of male-female partnership?

What Men Want You to Know about Them

Don't you wish you could climb inside guys' minds to see what they're thinking? We do, too—so we asked some.

We asked a handful of men in youth ministry to answer a few key questions about women in youth ministry. No matter what your background, odds are good that the men you work with share some of the same opinions. In fact, maybe you should ask them these same questions and see for yourself. It could be the start of a great conversation.

1. Women in youth ministry would be surprised if they realized men...

...don't really think they have all the answers...they just act like it! LOL :^)

Aaron, Arizona

...are the most insecure mammals on the planet. You can help us by not overreacting to our little temper tantrums and by not treating us like little boys, even though we may be acting like it. Also, men fight and then go have a beer together...often our disagreement is not personal, it is ideological. Don't take what we say to heart as an offense to your self-worth!

Dan, Colorado

...knew they could not bear the fruit that God had intended in a specific ministry without women serving alongside them. This generation of students is not looking for the out-going, guitar playing, long-winded male pastor to lead them into the presence of God. What they are looking for is a person who has no ego, who is not tied to a position, but rather someone they can sit down and talk with and who will listen first and give advice only when asked.

Wayne, Calgary, Canada

....aren't really surprised by your talents and abilities at all! They've known all along you are gifted.

Mike, California

...want so much for women to succeed in student ministry. Many men understand women's often untapped potential in leadership, ministry, teaching, relationship nurturing, planning, vision casting...you get the idea.

Al, Minnesota

...need partners of equal standing to model what it means to be godly women. While the competencies of men vary according to giftedness, one deficiency common to all men is their inability to be women. Go figure!

Gregg, Wisconsin

...are mostly clueless when in comes to how to handle a tenth-grade girl's issues at school or an eighth grader who is distraught about a boy who doesn't like her or a senior who "really loves this guy"...

Jake, Minnesota

2. Without women in youth ministry...

...there is a hole, something missing, it is incomplete. I fully believe that in the postmodern church we need women working alongside men. Just the other day I was talking with some students who asked, "Why don't we see women in front of our church?" These young women need to know that they are gifted just as men are.

Aaron, Arizona

...my last 12 years would not have been as fruitful or success-ful for my ministry. I have hired more women than men in my ministry career and have never regretted hiring a woman. Besides the obvious of being there for female students, women in youth ministry bring a balance and practical thinking to each area that concerns students. Many students under my leadership would have never found hope and heal-ing in their lives if it were not for a woman who was called by God to love students unconditionally.

Wayne, Calgary, Canada

...girls would grow up believing that they are not free to touch the lives of teenagers for Jesus. Without women in youth ministry, we would be vetoing God's spiritual gift-giving.

Jim, Hawaii

...we would not be giving God our best.

Al, Minnesota

...the wheels would fall off. There is no question that women have always played a critical role in youth ministry. In Micah 6:8, it tells us that God requires us to do justly, love mercy, and walk humbly with our God. Without women in ministry, the "do justly" dominates over the "love mercy," and the necessary humility is significantly diminished. Together our youth ministry programs become much more obedient to God's calling.

Mark, Colorado

3. One thing I'd like to change for women in youth ministry is...

...I think Paul's writings have forever damaged many women's perception of the legitimacy of their call to ministry. This is unfortunate, and in my humble opinion, lousy exegetical work. This is a loss, and it is up to men and women in the kingdom who have a different view to begin to correctly help all people find their place in ministry.

Dan, Colorado

...that they didn't have to work twice as hard to get half the credit men get.

Wayne, Calgary, Canada

...that the clergy playing field was more level. While some seminaries will intentionally admit an equal gender ratio, churches in most denominations aren't hiring women to be pastors as fast or as often as men.

Jim, Hawaii

...to create greater numbers of significant ministry opportunities for them. I would also like to see more men providing these opportunities and not be threatened by their influence.

Mike, California

...to see more female mentors for them. It just seems like it's difficult to find many (I know there are some) of those veteran women who have journeyed far with God in ministry and have seen and heard and done things that younger women could benefit from learning.

Al, Minnesota

...is to remove the "beauty is power" clause in our culture's definition of who is important and why. We are fixated on external beauty as a culture. And unfortunately it is just as true inside the church.

I recently heard of a ministry in Florida that called a friend of mine for a reference on a female youth pastor. He was asked, "How does she look in a bathing suit?"

"What?" asked my friend.

"You're a guy; you understand," came the reply. "We are a beach church, and we have to consider these things."

Mark, Colorado

...the gnawing urge to feel like they have to be more like men to validate their presence and effectiveness. Their femininity is a God-designed asset to any comprehensive youth ministry.

Gregg, Wisconsin

...I would get rid of the stigma that we can only have paid staff be men. My dream team for student ministry is all about having ladies on staff! The other thing I would change is for the women in youth ministry to realize they cannot be nearly as effective in the lives of the boys as men can. So if you are a woman running a program or in leadership, you need to have some dyno-mite male staff (volunteer or paid) that come alongside you to connect with the guys and love up on them.

Jake, Minnesota

4. I would want to encourage women in youth ministry by telling them...

...to hang in there. There is a place for you, and the tide is changing. More and more congregations are becoming open to the idea of women working as volunteers and full- or part-time student ministers.

Aaron, Arizona

...you are a child of God, no more and no less important than your male counterpart. Please don't let your gender sway you from your calling. May it be a gift that you bring to the table to be used by the King.

Dan, Colorado

...the heart and spirit that women bring to youth ministry are incredibly valued and needed, more than men will ever admit. Youth ministry is a principle-based approach to seeing students grow in their faith, but the Christian church has made it a personality-based or gender-based issue that it shouldn't be.

Wayne, Calgary, Canada

...a girl in my youth group told me she was inspired by a woman who was serving as an associate pastor at our church.

"Have you talked to her?" I asked.

"No," she said, "I just like knowing I could be one."

Women in ministry are making a difference for students that they may not even see.

Jim, Hawaii

...it's your turn! Find a place in ministry where you and your talents are appreciated and valued, and where your gifts not only impact the lives of the girls in your group, but also the young men.

Mike, California

...they are bringing balance to a "profession" that has been way too male for way too long. Youth programs in general have been strong on "fight and conquer" and poor on "love and encourage." Please continue to bring your compassionate hearts into the teenage world that is so harsh and unforgiving.

Mark, Colorado

...the power to transform young lives is not gender-specific. It lies in the Word of God, empowered by the Spirit of God, not within us or our personal performance. None of us are competent in and of ourselves to accomplish anything of lasting value in youth ministry. Apart from Christ I can do nothing (John 15:5), but with God all things are possible (Matthew 19:26). Even Paul said, "Not that we are competent in ourselves to claim anything for ourselves, but our competence comes from God" (2 Corinthians 3:5). The wonder of it all is that God chooses to use us as his "agents of change" entrusted with everyday opportunities to leave a personal mark on eternity.

Gregg, Wisconsin

Thanks. We couldn't have said it better ourselves.

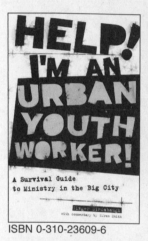

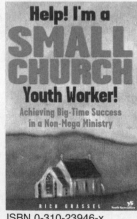
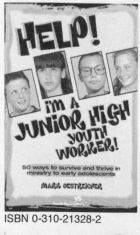

It's finally here—
a comprehensive tool to help you get, and stay, organized!

If you're like most youth workers, the least favorite part of your job is the myriad of administrative and operational details you have to keep track of. This resource is what you need to find quick and accessible answers to your management, administrative, and supervisory questions and needs. Complete with CD-ROM that allows you to customize forms, checklists and samples you'll find exactly what your looking for to organize and manage your ministry.

Also includes The Youth Assistant®/Special Edition, the popular student contact database that organizes and gives you instant access to birthdays, lables, events, notes, mail merge, as well as student volunteer, small group, and visitor info.

Download a sample at www.youthspecialties.com/store
Search by title and click "Sample"
Order online or visit your local Christian Bookstore

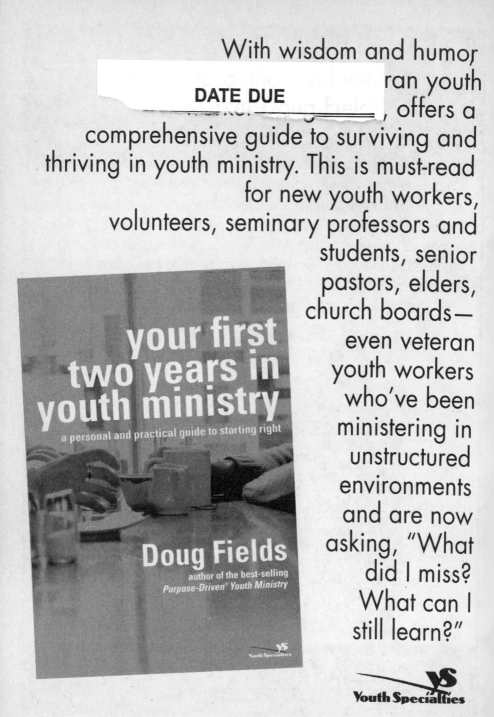